BORN READING

20 STORIES OF WOMEN READING THEIR WAY INTO HISTORY

KATHLEEN KRULL AND VIRGINIA LOH-HAGAN · ILLUSTRATED BY AURA LEWIS

A PAULA WISEMAN BOOK

Simon & Schuster Books for Young Readers • New York London Toronto Sydney New Delhi

This book is dedicated to my dear friend, piano nerd,
fellow reader, and author mentor, Kathleen Krull.
—V. L.-H.

To Sharon, Maya, Yahli, Roee, Peleg,
and Sebastian, with love.
—A. L.

SIMON & SCHUSTER BOOKS FOR YOUNG READERS
An imprint of Simon & Schuster Children's Publishing Division
1230 Avenue of the Americas, New York, New York 10020
Text © 2023 by Estate of Kathleen Krull and Virginia Loh-Hagan
Jacket illustration © 2023 by Aura Lewis
Jacket design by Sarah Creech © 2023 by Simon & Schuster, Inc.
Interior illustration © 2023 by Aura Lewis
SIMON & SCHUSTER BOOKS FOR YOUNG READERS and related marks are trademarks of Simon & Schuster, Inc.
For information about special discounts for bulk purchases, please contact Simon & Schuster
Special Sales at 1-866-506-1949 or business@simonandschuster.com.
The Simon & Schuster Speakers Bureau can bring authors to your live event. For more information or to book an event, contact the Simon &
Schuster Speakers Bureau at 1-866-248-3049 or visit our website at www.simonspeakers.com.
Interior design by Sarah Creech and Alicia Mikles
The text for this book was set in Sabon.
The illustrations for this book were rendered digitally.
Manufactured in China
0423 SCP
First Edition
2 4 6 8 10 9 7 5 3 1
Library of Congress Cataloging-in-Publication Data
Names: Krull, Kathleen, author. | Loh-Hagan, Virginia, author. | Lewis, Aura, illustrator.
Title: Born reading : 20 stories of women reading their way into history / Kathleen Krull and Virginia Loh-Hagan ; illustrated by Aura Lewis.
Description: First edition. | New York : Simon & Schuster Books for Young Readers, [2023] | Includes bibliographical references.
Audience: Ages 8-12. | Audience: Grades 7-9. | Summary: "Once books change their brains, girls change history. Discover the foundation
of reading that empowered some of the world's most influential women in this collection of 20 biographies"— Provided by publisher.
Identifiers: LCCN 2022028198 (print) | LCCN 2022028199 (ebook) | ISBN 9781665917988 (hardcover) | ISBN 9781665917995 (ebook)
Subjects: LCSH: Women—Books and reading—History—Juvenile literature. | Women—Biography—Juvenile literature.
Classification: LCC Z1039.W65 K78 2023 (print) | LCC Z1039.W65 (ebook) | DDC 028/.9082 [B]—dc23/eng/20220701
LC record available at https://lccn.loc.gov/2022028198
LC ebook record available at https://lccn.loc.gov/2022028199

CONTENTS

Note from Virginia Loh-Hagan: When Kathleen Krull started this book, she had already written three profiles: Cleopatra, Sonia Sotomayor, and Serena Williams. I kept most of her writing intact. However, edits were respectfully made for clarity and coherence.

# INTRODUCTION

Books are powerful tools for equity and liberation. They allow readers to imagine different lives. They promote ideas like freedom and justice. They encourage the questioning of our lives and actions. Reading and having access to books are privileges that should not be taken lightly. Not everyone had or has such access. The last thing a patriarchal society wants is for women to question their positions in society. Throughout history and even today, women have been denied the right to read. But women have fought and continue to fight back. Women have read on, and they continue to do so.

Girls who read have become women who lead. For many girls, reading is a means of self-education and empowerment. It has lifted them out of poverty and/or obscurity. From reading books, women have learned new skills and gained new ways of thinking. They have started their own businesses. They have run for elected office. They have educated and uplifted their communities. They have written their own stories.

This book is a collection of little-known stories of influential women and their love for reading. In many ways these women were born reading. Their love for reading inspired them to do great things. This anthology features a select group of important women, but there are many, many other women who are both readers and leaders.

Reading changes hearts and minds, and the history of women reading tells a story of women gaining power. On women reading, author Kathleen Krull said, "Once books change their brains, girls change history."

CLEOPATRA LIVES IN THE LIBRARY
CLEOPATRA (69–30 BC)

"I will not be triumphed over."

(Quote attributed to Cleopatra by ancient Roman historian Livy)

For ordinary girls in ancient Egypt, education was considered a waste. They were trained at home by their mothers in sewing, cooking, and other skills needed for being a wife and mother. Cleopatra, who was anything but an ordinary girl, was destined for much more—she ruled ancient Egypt for over two decades and secured ancient Egypt's place in history as a world power.

Cleopatra had the great good fortune to be born into a royal family. Only royal daughters received an education in reading and writing, equal to what royal sons learned. They needed to be able to help their male family members lead and fend off rivals. As such, Cleopatra was educated on politics, history, science (including astronomy), math, music and the other arts, and languages. She loved learning. She hung out by herself for long hours in the fabled library of Alexandria, the greatest in the world. She practically lived in the library. She read hundreds of books in the form of papyrus scrolls, her mind working a mile a minute, sensing that all this learning would surely enhance her power. She had Plans (with a capital *P*).

Cleopatra's first language was Greek. Her tutors helped her absorb the lessons in each of Aesop's fables, amusing stories that use talking animals to show how to behave ethically. She went on to read *The Iliad* and *The Odyssey*, epic poems by Homer about gods and heroes with noble themes, like achieving heroism in battle. Then she read all the famous Greek plays and philosophical works, which included *Prometheus Bound* by Aeschylus, *The*

Frogs by Aristophanes, and *The Republic* by Plato. It made sense that Cleopatra learned Greek first, as she was descended from a line of Ptolemaic pharaohs. The Ptolemaic dynasty was a Macedonian Greek royal family that ruled ancient Egypt for about 275 years. These rulers spoke Greek and refused to learn the native Egyptian language, which was too complex for them to bother to learn. But Cleopatra was different. She learned to speak and read Egyptian. She was the first Ptolemaic ruler to learn the Egyptian language. She did not want to have to rely on others to interpret what Egyptians were saying. This endeared her to the Egyptian people.

She clearly had a gift for languages. Legend is that she could speak at least nine of them. In addition to Greek and Egyptian, she learned Latin, Ethiopian, Hebrew, Arabic, and others. An ancient historian said, "It was a pleasure merely to hear the sound of her voice, with which, like an instrument of many strings, she could pass from one language to another." Plutarch, a Greek philosopher and historian, commented on her ability to also speak the "language of flattery." Cleopatra was able to charm people to do her bidding.

Cleopatra was ambitious. She knew she wanted to rule, but gaining the throne was not an easy feat. Her family members married one another to keep their power and to keep their royal bloodline "pure." At the age of eighteen, Cleopatra married her ten-year-old brother and ensured she'd become queen of Egypt. But their marriage was not a happy one. She was a terrible wife and a terrible big sister. She found her brother to be an obstacle to her ruling in her own right. There were rumors that Cleopatra may have been involved in the drowning of her husband-brother and the poisoning of another brother. With her brothers out of the way, Cleopatra was able to rise to power.

As queen, Cleopatra became the richest woman in the world, and she lived well. But she had a job to do. Rome wanted to take Egypt's place as the world's greatest superpower, and it was up to Cleopatra to stop this from happening. She wanted to avoid war with the mighty Roman Empire and sought to build an alliance. Her talent for languages came in handy during diplomatic negotiations. She had no trouble communicating with other rulers, especially with Roman rulers. Fending off a Roman invasion, she was able to pursue her goal: ruling the entire world (while continuing to read).

Sometimes Cleopatra took her love of reading a little too far—she invaded other lands just to loot their libraries. She brought home yet more books, increasing her collection at the world-famous library in Alexandria. She spent much of her time alone there, reading her treasured books. Some historians have suggested that she was more than just a reader and may have even written her own literary contribution: a book about cosmetics. She was always playing around with makeup, hairstyles, and new perfumes. She had many ideas and tips on beauty and fashion—for example, bathing in donkey's milk and applying aloe vera leaves to the skin.

Cleopatra's library was a jewel of the ancient Mediterranean world. For many, it was the center of intellectual life. For Cicero, an ancient Roman politician, it was a source of great envy. Cicero prided himself on his own personal library. Knowing that Cleopatra, a woman, had a better library, and thus was possibly more educated than him, offended him. He was also offended when he asked to borrow a book from Cleopatra's library and she never followed through. He stated, "I detest the queen."

Marc Antony, the great Roman general and leader, won her heart by gifting her with new scrolls for her library. Antony and Cleopatra embarked upon one of the greatest love affairs of all time. In addition to being extremely fond of each other, they also needed each other, politically. Cleopatra needed Antony to protect her crown and secure Egypt's role as a world power. Antony needed Cleopatra to give him access to Egypt's riches and resources. In general, though, they enjoyed each other's company, often traveling, feasting, and fighting together. But the key to their success was spending hours together in the library.

In 30 BC, Antony and Cleopatra were being threatened by Roman armies that were suspicious of Antony's close ties to Egypt. To avoid losing their power and each other, they took their own lives. Antony, thinking Cleopatra had died, stabbed himself in the stomach; his lifeless body was taken to Cleopatra. Heartbroken about Antony and refusing to be taken to Rome as a prisoner, Cleopatra, it's believed, died by poisoning herself with snake venom. But according to Plutarch, "What really took place is known to no one." Antony and Cleopatra were buried together in Cleopatra's tomb. When she died at age thirty-nine, no one could replace her. The days of Egyptian independence were over. Cleopatra's children were sent to Rome, so without any heirs, Cleopatra became the last of her family to rule. Thus, Egypt became a province of the Roman Empire.

History has painted Cleopatra as someone who used her "looks" to get what she wanted. It is common for women's accomplishments to be belittled in such a way. There was no doubt that Cleopatra knew how to use her looks. She had a flair for drama and used pageantry to her advantage. But Cleopatra, like the best of books, should not be judged by her cover. Underestimating her cleverness and political savviness, as history and men have done, is a huge mistake. Cleopatra was a force to be reckoned with. She was an ambitious political genius and defiantly well read. An effective leader, she secured Egypt's status as a dominant force in the ancient world. As the last true pharaoh of Egypt, she remains the most famous woman ruler in history.

WU GETS AHEAD

WU ZETIAN (624–705)

"Compassion gives rise to good fortune."

Wu Zetian, the first and only woman emperor of China, was known as many things. She was mainly known by her own surname, Wu, and not by her husband's name. In Chinese *wu* means "warrior," and Wu was definitely a fierce fighter. She let nothing get in the way of her rise to the top. She ascended at a time when a woman's greatest role in the empire was to bear heirs. She was not supposed to interfere in the affairs of the state, and she was definitely not supposed to rule. But she did. A controversial figure, she was known for being ambitious and ruthless, accused of committing adultery, torture, murder, and infanticide. At the same time she was known as an effective ruler who ushered her country into a golden age of peace and prosperity. During her rule China became the most cosmopolitan of the world's major empires. Trade via the Silk Road was at its peak, giving Wu access to the world and great riches.

Wu refused to conform to the gender expectations of her time; because of that, she was able to advance far more than most women could in a world made for men. She used books to gain power. A stubborn child, she spurned traditional female hobbies and preferred to read instead. Born into a rich and noble family, Wu had access to books. Her father strongly encouraged her to get educated, which was not a common practice. With her father's support, Wu faced no obstacles to her education. She took it upon herself to learn about all different types of topics, including literature, politics, history, and music.

At age fourteen she was selected to be one of Emperor Taizong's many royal mistresses. Her main responsibility was to do Taizong's personal laundry, which she used as a way to get closer to Taizong. Whenever she was in his room with him, she would chat him up. A

known beauty, Wu surprised Taizong with her brains. Taizong was so wooed by her intellect that he promoted her to become his assistant. Wu was permitted to work in the imperial study, where she read official documents and gained a knowledge of state affairs at the highest levels. She read and learned how to govern a country.

Upon Taizong's death Wu was sent to a Buddhist monastery. As per custom, it would be an insult to the deceased ruler if she were to marry another. Mistresses who did not bear any sons were supposed to shave their heads, live in confinement, and pray for their dead husband's soul. Such a life was not for Wu. She escaped from the monastery and returned to court by bribing officials. She defied all her naysayers and enemies by making her way back into court life. One historical source referred to her as having "the heart of a serpent and the nature of a wolf." Once again, she used her wit and intellect to woo the new ruler, Emperor Gaozong. It is believed she wrote him a poem: "Watching red turn to green, my thoughts entangled and scattered, / I am disheveled and torn from my longing for you, my lord."

Wu became Gaozong's empress. Lucky for Wu, Gaozong turned out to be an incompetent leader. In addition, he had bad eyesight and struggled to read. So Wu read all the official documents and ruled in his stead. After Gaozong's death Wu ruled through her sons, who were also incompetent, lacking the leadership skills and intellect needed to effectively govern. Eventually, Wu ruled in her own right, declaring herself to be the emperor. Although being a woman made her suspicious, there was no doubt she knew what she was doing. She maintained power and eliminated opposition by having a system of spies and secret police.

She also ruled by ensuring that the common people had greater access to books and education. T. H. Barrett, a leading scholar of medieval China, has suggested that Wu was an early adopter of the concept of the printing press, which would allow for mass dissemination of texts. She was also a publisher. She published books about rules for officials. She published a collection of biographies of famous women, asserting that the ideal ruler was one who ruled as a mother does over her children. She published farming textbooks. She also wrote poems and essays. She created new characters for the Chinese writing system to demonstrate her power in being able to change the words people used. She understood that changing how people talk leads to changing how they think. Today these characters are known as "Zetian characters."

Wu was famous for yielding great power. According to court rumors and stories, she was believed to rule over even nature. In the dead of winter she walked in her garden and recited the following poem: "Tomorrow morning I will roam the imperial garden / With great dispatch let spring be informed. / The flowers must bloom overnight / Without waiting for the morning zephyrs to blow." The next morning all the flowers bloomed. For many in her court, this was proof of her power.

She was also an early adopter of Buddhism, which was more friendly to women than Confucianism. She built temples so that priests could explain Buddhist texts to common people. Going against Confucian patriarchal ideals, Wu was seen as a disrupter and a freak of nature. She never consulted with Confucian scholars and criticized Confucian beliefs about the superiority of men over women. This made others skeptical of her—many challenged her authority. Applying Buddhist principles, Wu sought to bring more equity into her society; in this way she was much more egalitarian and compassionate than her predecessors. For example, she supported a system of examinations for military jobs instead of just appointing noblemen. She valued education and intellect over aristocratic connections.

She was trashed in the news of the time by some of her subjects who found her boldness to be unusual and unsettling. Like many women in power, she suffered from gossip, slander, and doubt. People constantly underestimated her ability to rule, simply because she was born a girl. She may have actually done the brutal things of which she was accused; but male rulers have done the same if not much worse. Yet, because she was female, her scandals often overshadowed her successes.

Wu died at the age of eighty-one. Even though she was an avid reader, there is nothing to read on her tombstone. It is the only known blank memorial in more than two thousand years of imperial Chinese history. Some historians see this as a sign of praise, in that her accomplishments were too many to be expressed in writing. Other historians see this as punishment for her overthrowing the traditional customs of male-dominated China. The real reason is unknown. But what is known is that the well-read Wu was a powerful world leader who protected and expanded China's empire.

ELIZABETH RULES THE DAY
QUEEN ELIZABETH I (1533–1603)

"I know I have the body of a weak and feeble woman,
but I have the heart and stomach of a king, and of a king of England too."

Queen Elizabeth I was one of England's greatest monarchs. She protected England from invasion, supported art and culture, and forged England as a strong and independent nation. But her life began with tragedy. Elizabeth's father, King Henry VIII, married six different women, one of whom was Elizabeth's mother, Anne Boleyn. When Elizabeth was two years old, Henry accused Anne of treason and adultery and had her beheaded. However, Anne's real crime was not bearing him any sons. Henry, obsessed with getting a male heir, found his daughter with Anne, Elizabeth, a female, to be a great disappointment.

Although Henry may not have been a doting father, he did make sure Elizabeth was well educated. Both Henry and Anne were intellects and spoke several languages. Elizabeth inherited his love of learning and gift for languages; she also inherited Henry's red hair. Of her father, she said, "I may not be a lion, but I am a lion's cub and I have a lion's heart." Learning alongside her half brother, Edward, who was the heir to the throne, Elizabeth received an education fit for a king. Soon after taking the throne, Edward died young, which eventually cleared the way for Elizabeth to become queen. At the age of twenty-five Elizabeth became queen of England, providing stability, peace, and prosperity for forty-four years. Her rule became known as the "Elizabethan era," which was a golden age for the arts. When she became queen, she said, "Though you have had, and may have, many princes more mighty and wise sitting in this seat, yet you never had, nor shall have, any that will be more careful and loving."

Elizabeth started her formal education at around age five. At this time most children's early education was overseen by their mothers. This was not an option for Elizabeth. So her first teacher was Kat Ashley, a well-educated English governess. Kat taught Elizabeth religion and courtly subjects such as manners, horse riding, hunting, dancing, music, and sewing. She also taught her academic subjects such as reading, writing, grammar, geography, math, astronomy, history, French, Italian, Flemish, and Spanish. Of Kat, Elizabeth said that she took "great labour and pain in bringing of me up in learning and honesty."

Elizabeth loved learning. At age eleven she wrote a letter to her stepmother, Catherine Parr, the last of Henry's six wives, saying, "Even as an instrument of iron or of other metal waxeth soon rusty unless it be continually occupied, even so shall the wit of a man or a woman wax dull and unapt to do or understand anything perfectly unless it be always occupied upon some manner of study." For her entire life Elizabeth was committed to her education. She wanted to be known for her intelligence and wit.

After Kat, Elizabeth's tutors were from Cambridge University, and they were among the great humanist scholars of the time. One of her teachers was Roger Ascham, who said of Elizabeth, "Her mind has no womanly weakness. Her perseverance is equal to that of a man." Although this comment is sexist, it was a compliment back in Elizabeth's day. Under Roger's tutelage Elizabeth studied classical subjects, including rhetoric, philosophy, and history. Her day started with reading the New Testament in Greek. Then she read and translated classical authors like Petrarch, Seneca, and Horace. She would first translate into English and then back into the original language. Elizabeth's afternoons were devoted to Latin, theology, and languages. After dinner she relaxed by rereading her favorite passages.

Roger noted she read more Greek in a day than most churchmen read Latin in a week. Elizabeth studied Greek texts closely and learned oration skills from them. A talented writer and speaker, she wrote and delivered her own speeches. She also wrote poetry and songs. Her obsession with Greek and Latin continued into her adulthood. When she became queen, she and Roger regularly set aside time to read their favorite classical authors together. Some reports indicate that she spent about three hours a day reading history.

Elizabeth prided herself on being well read and well informed. She loved reading about gossip from around the globe. To both entertain her and win her favor, ambassadors would include "merry tales" in their reports. She loved saying, "I know more than thou dost." She also had excellent memory skills. She was a regular reader of scripture, especially the Psalms. Whenever possible, she liked to show off by making witty remarks and reciting quotes. For fun, Elizabeth liked to translate books. This was her way to de-stress and take a break from her queenly duties. She translated several texts that were gifted to her step-mother, Catherine.

Elizabeth was known for always carrying a book with her. In fact, the earliest surviving portrait of her was painted a year before her father died. The artist, William Scrots, pictured a young Elizabeth with a book in her hand and a larger book on a stand next to her. The portrait is described as "the picture of the Lady Elizabeth her grace with a book in her hand, her gown like crimson cloth." Elizabeth approved of this likeness, as she was a proud book nerd. Of this portrait, she wrote, "For the face I grant I might well blush to offer, but the mind I shall never be ashamed to present." Elizabeth cared more about what people thought about her intelligence than her looks.

Queen Elizabeth I was an exemplary politician, orator, and musician. Under her rule England emerged as a world power. She unified a Protestant England against the Catholic Spanish, defeated the Spanish Armada, developed effective legal institutions, expanded the British Empire by colonizing lands overseas, and promoted the arts. As a woman, she defied perceptions of the time and showed the world that she was a formidable leader. She said, "Though the sex to which I belong is considered weak, you will nevertheless find me a rock that bends to no wind."

Elizabeth was strong and witty until the end. During her final days, when she appeared to be sickly, one of her advisers said that she "must go to bed." She responded, "Little man, the word 'must' is never used to princes." She always had the last word.

JUANA READS IN SECRET

SOR (SISTER) JUANA INÉS DE LA CRUZ (1651–1695)

"I don't study to know more, but to ignore less."

In addition to being a nun, Sor (Sister) Juana Inés de la Cruz was a well-known and well-respected Mexican poet, writer, scholar, composer, and feminist. Because she was born out of wedlock to a Spanish father (who abandoned her at a young age) and a mother who was a "criolla" (a person of European Spanish descent but born in the Americas), she was officially registered as a "daughter of the Church" and was socially ostracized. Though she faced much prejudice, she luckily grew up on her wealthy maternal grandfather's estate outside of Mexico City, where she found safety in books.

A child prodigy, she was reading and writing at a young age. "I was not yet three years old when my mother determined to send one of my elder sisters to learn to read at a school for girls," she said. "Affection and mischief caused me to follow her, and when I observed how she was being taught her lessons I was so inflamed with the desire to know how to read." Juana convinced the teacher to teach her to read as well. A quick learner, she was reading fluently before her mother found out she had been sneaking out to go to school. In addition to Spanish, Juana also learned to read and write in Nahuatl, an Aztec language spoken in Central Mexico.

Even though Juana lived at a time when women were not encouraged to be educated, her entire life consisted of self-study. "Who has forbidden women to engage in private and individual studies? Have they not a rational soul as men do?" she asked. "I have this inclination to study and if it is evil, I am not the one who formed me thus—I was born with it and with it, I shall die." Juana cared more about learning than anything else. She said, "I do

not set store by treasures or riches. And, therefore, it always brings me more joy only to fix riches in my intellect. And never my intellect to fix on riches."

All she needed was books and a quiet place to read. Fortunately, her grandfather was a huge reader with tables and shelves overflowing with books. He also had a library and chapel right next to each other. Juana would secretly get books from her grandfather's library and then hide in the chapel for hours reading them. She made a nest of books around her. She read anything she could get her hands on. She said, "There were not enough punishments, or reprimands, to prevent me from reading." At age eight Juana wrote a poem for a contest at church and won. Guess what her prize was? A book! She was well on her way to starting her own library.

To her great dismay, she wasn't allowed to attend the university, which was accessible only to males at that time. She begged her mother to let her disguise herself as a boy, but her mother didn't approve. So, once again, Juana read in secret and educated herself. She said, "Study and more study, with no teachers but my books. Thus, I learned how difficult it is to study those soulless letters, lacking a human voice or the explication of a teacher. . . . I undertook this great task [of self-study] without benefit of teacher, or fellow students with whom to confer and discuss, having for a master no other than a mute book, and for a colleague, an insentient inkwell."

When her grandfather died, her mother wanted to give the precocious Juana more opportunities. She sent her to live in Mexico City with her maternal aunt and uncle. Juana was excited about the move, as Mexico City was the bustling cosmopolitan center of New Spain's colonial world. She continued her self-education there. She learned Greek and struggled with Latin, for which her relatives secured a tutor for her. Determined to conquer the language, she would cut off her hair every time she made a mistake in Latin. She vowed to master Latin before letting her hair grow out. She said, "It turned out that the hair grew quickly, and I learned slowly. As a result, I cut off the hair in punishment for my head's ignorance, for it didn't seem right to me that a head so naked of knowledge should be dressed up with hair, for knowledge is a more desirable adornment."

Because her relatives were well connected, her love of learning was well known. She caught the attention of the viceroy and his wife, who had heard about her intelligence and invited her to court. She was tested by a panel of scholars who interrogated her with question after question. She gave such a stellar performance that she became a bit of a celebrity at court. As an intellect, however, Juana found court life to be distracting—plus, she kept getting annoying marriage proposals, all of which she turned down. At twenty years old, when most women were married off, Juana went her own way. She chose to become a nun, as this was the only way she could study as she wished (without men around to bug her). She said she wanted "to have no fixed occupation which might curtail my freedom to study."

At her convent she thrived (at least in the beginning). She had her own study and created her own library of over four thousand books. She had a tiny room filled with books, scientific instruments, and maps. She hosted salons where she engaged in deep conversations with other intellectuals and nobles. She wrote poetry, carols, plays, and essays that were widely read. Although she was tucked away in a convent, she found great freedom in learning. As she put it, "Nothing enjoys greater freedom than the human understanding."

Given Sor Juana's rebellious streak, it is no surprise that a patriarchal society and strict religious orders found her to be a bit controversial. She read and wrote about all types of topics, not just religious ones. A forward thinker, she wrote about taboo themes such as romantic love and feminism. Some historical records indicate that she had a love affair with a countess who was one of her patrons. In fact, her works included lesbian love poetry. For example: "That you're a woman far away / is no hindrance to my love: / for the soul, as you well know, / distance and sex don't count." Some historians refer to her as North America's first lesbian feminist writer.

But Juana's greatest controversy (and alleged crime) centered on her criticism of religion and religious figures of the time. She had accused the church and the state of being biased against women. She consistently argued that her love of learning was a part of God's plan, which she presented as proof that God supported women's education. Her most known work is her "Response to Sister Filotea" in which she defended a woman's right to study and teach, condemning the church for keeping women uneducated. She said, "God graced me with a gift of an immense love for the truth." She believed the key to girls' education is more educated women, since "one can perfectly well philosophize while cooking supper. . . . If more women teach, maybe young girls could learn without being harassed so much."

Needless to say, her feminist, progressive beliefs were not well received by church officials, who were male. These male officials, representing the church, banned the reading of her work. To these men, she wrote, "You always are so foolish / Your censure is unfair." Sor Juana was censored and forced into a life of recluse and silence. She was pressured to renounce her intellectual pursuits, to retract her criticisms, and to conform to church life. As a result of this pressure, she stopped reading nonreligious texts and no longer published her work. To add insult to injury, Juana was forced to give away her library of books, which must have felt like a stab to the heart. Sor Juana, tired of fighting the patriarchy and nearing the last years of her life, had committed herself to a life of charity—she abided by church laws and gave up reading and writing. She died when a plague hit the convent.

But her impact lives on. People continue to read her writings and study her life. As a hometown heroine, she is featured on the 200 peso note in Mexico. In addition, her convent, in which she lived for more than twenty-five years, is now the University of the Cloister of Sor Juana. A girl who was forbidden to go to school now has a school named after her.

PHILLIS USES HER VOICE

PHILLIS WHEATLEY PETERS (1753–1784)

"In every human Breast, God has implanted a Principle, which we call Love of Freedom;

it is impatient of Oppression, and pants for Deliverance."

Phillis Wheatley Peters was one of the best-known poets in eighteenth-century America. Her poetry was known to be progressive and emotional. In addition, she challenged the racist assumptions and ideologies of her day.

She wrote of her own traumatic past under the brutal institution of American slavery: "I, young in life, by seeming cruel fate / Was snatch'd from Africa's fancy'd happy seat." Stolen from the Senegambia region in West Africa, she was brought on a slave ship to Boston, Massachusetts, in 1761. The slave ship was named the *Phillis*. It carried ninety-five enslaved people; only seventy-five survived the journey. John and Susanna Wheatley, wealthy merchants, bought Phillis "for a trifle" and named her after the slave ship. Phillis was about the same age as their young daughter who had recently passed away. She was described as a "slender, frail female child" who was "evidently suffering from a change of climate." She was naked with "no other covering than a quantity of dirty carpet about her." The only existing account of her forced arrival describes her as being "about seven years old . . . from the circumstance of shedding her front teeth." Sickly, Phillis was not expected to live long; she suffered from asthma her entire life.

Phillis was bought to serve as Susanna's companion and servant. But she turned out to be a quick learner, impressing Susanna with her skills. She was found copying the English alphabet on a wall in chalk. Regarded as a prodigy, she was relieved from most of her domestic duties and was allowed the opportunity to learn. She was taught by Susanna and her elder daughter, Mary. As a reward for being a top student, she was given a dictionary, a room of her own to read and write, and a fire and all the candles she needed for light. Phillis was taught several subjects, including reading, writing, religion, Latin, Greek, and ancient history.

Within sixteen months of her arrival, Phillis was reading the Bible, Greek and Latin classics, and British literature. She preferred adult works of literature over children's books. Her favorite authors were Homer, Virgil, Alexander Pope, John Milton, and other classic poets. She also studied history, politics, astronomy, and geography. She spent her day reading, writing, and sewing.

At a young age Phillis began writing poetry. She wanted to publish her work and hoped the Wheatleys would use their connections to help her. At around age fourteen in 1767, she published her first poem in a Rhode Island weekly newspaper. Her poem was entitled "On Messrs. Hussey and Coffin" and was about two men who nearly drowned at sea. She was inspired to write this poem after two guests of the Wheatleys recounted their sea adventures over dinner.

Phillis published more poems in local newspapers and became a local celebrity. Readers were impressed by her use of sound, color, and rhythm. But Phillis faced much prejudice. Some critics were skeptical that an enslaved person could write at all. It was not common for enslaved people to be educated at this time. In some states, especially in the South, educating enslaved people was illegal and punishable. Education endangered the system of slavery, as it enabled the enslaved people to read about abolition and to learn ways to escape. Phillis helped to dismantle the low opinions white Americans at that time had of Black people, who were assumed to lack intelligence. Dehumanizing and diminishing Black people and Indigenous people was a strategy used to justify slavery. Phillis was aware that she was given more access to education than other Black people, which was the reason for her advanced scholarship. Although she was praised for and benefited from her education, she recognized that Colonial America was racist and saw herself not as an example, but as an exception. "The world is a severe schoolmaster," she observed, "for its frowns are less dangerous than its smiles and flatteries, and it is a difficult task to keep in the path of wisdom."

When Phillis tried to publish a book of poems, one of her main obstacles was that people didn't believe she wrote it. They assumed a white man was most likely doing the writing. Phillis had to prove she was the writer by getting examined by at least fifteen of Boston's most notable white men, including John Hancock, who interrogated her and gave her a series of questions and tasks to demonstrate that she could read and write. For Phillis, this must have been humiliating and maddening at the same time. Eventually, these men signed a letter confirming that Phillis was, indeed, literate. Despite this letter, there were many people who still doubted Phillis's abilities.

Since America was not ready to publish a book by an enslaved Black girl, Phillis sought other opportunities. Funded by the Wheatleys, she went to London and became a big hit. She found a patron, or financial sponsor, and was able to get her first collection of poems published in 1773. Her book became the first book published by an African American author. Dr. Henry Louis Gates Jr., a renowned scholar of African American literature, wrote, "Phillis Wheatley almost immediately became the most famous African on the face of the earth." Phillis was a shrewd bookseller. For example, she signed copies to avoid loss of profits due to pirated editions. Her London trip was cut short when Susanna fell ill. Phillis returned to Massachusetts to care for Susanna and to seek her emancipation, which was granted soon after her book was published.

Phillis used her writing as a way to voice her opposition and resistance to slavery. She wrote letters to important figures fighting for liberty and freedom. She even wrote several poems about George Washington: "Proceed, great chief, with virtue on thy side / Thy ev'ry action let the goddess guide." What's more, Washington actually replied to one of her letters: "I thank you most sincerely for your polite notice of me, in the elegant lines you enclosed . . . the style and manner exhibit a striking proof of your great poetical talents." He was so impressed by her that he invited her to visit him; little is known about their conversation, but it can be assumed that their meeting was polite and cordial on the basis of their mutual admiration. Phillis hoped that freedom for the colonies would also mean freedom for the enslaved.

In 1778 Phillis married John Peters, a free Black man from Boston. Phillis and John shared a love for reading. (In fact, upon his death John's only possessions consisted of a Bible and thirteen other books.) In future writings Phillis identified herself as "Phillis Peters," shedding her former enslaver's name.

Phillis kept writing, but unfortunately, her efforts to publish a second book of poems failed. As the colonies were engaging in the Revolutionary War to gain independence from England, Phillis was unable to enact her previous strategy of getting published in England due to rising tensions between the two lands. Through her writings, she was an ardent and public supporter of American independence and thus was not seen favorably in England. In addition, racism still stood in the way of Phillis getting published in the colonies, where African Americans were seen as property and a labor source.

Because of a war that depleted money and resources, times were tough. Phillis spent her last years in poverty. As free Black people, Phillis and John had a hard time competing with white business owners. John was sent to jail for debt, and Phillis was forced to work as a maid. Despite that, as she was both an artist and an intellectual, she continued to read and write poetry. She referred to herself as "the languid muse" blessed by "the celestial nine" who had given her a poetic voice; she wrote, "O'er me methought they deign'd to shine / And deign'd to string my lyre." She thanked the gods for giving her time to shine and talents to share.

Phillis's poetry is still widely read today. Although some of her writings are lost, scholars have uncovered many of her poems and letters. As the mother of the African American literary tradition, Phillis inspired other African Americans to find their voices and to create in spite of the limits placed on them. She said, "Enlarge the close contracted mind, / And fill it with thy fire."

E. PAULINE TAKES THE STAGE

E. PAULINE JOHNSON (1861–1913)

"Women are fonder of me than men are. I have had none fail me,
and I hope I have failed none. It is a keen pleasure for me to meet a congenial woman,
one that I feel will understand me, and will in turn let me peep into her own life—having confidence
in me, that is one of the dearest things between friends, strangers, acquaintances, or kindred."

Emily Pauline Johnson was an Indigenous Canadian poet, artist, and performer. She was born on the Six Nations Reserve near Brantford in Ontario, Canada. She was the daughter of a Mohawk chief and a descendant of one of the fifty noble families of the Iroquois Confederacy. (The Mohawk tribe is known as the "Keeper of the Eastern Door" in the Iroquois Confederacy. This means they are responsible for defending the confederacy against invasions from other tribes coming from the east in present-day New Brunswick in Canada and in New England states in the United States.) Her mother was an Englishwoman who immigrated to North America. As a girl of mixed ancestry, E. Pauline was born into a world that didn't always accept her, and she faced discrimination as a woman and as an Indigenous person.

Many of her works expressed the tensions of being between two cultures. She wrote, "The Paleface is a man of many moods; what he approves today he will disapprove tomorrow. . . . We of the ancient Iroquois can but little understand this strange mode of government." E. Pauline struggled with the contrasting treatment of women in her two cultures. "I have heard that the daughters of this vast city cry out for a voice in the Parliament of this land," she said. "There is no need for an Iroquois woman to clamor for recognition in our councils. . . . The highest title known to us is that of 'chief matron.' It is borne by the oldest woman of each of the noble families. . . . There are fifty matrons possessing this right in the Iroquois Confederacy. I have not

yet heard of fifty white women even among those of noble birth who may speak and be listened to in the lodge of the lawmakers here."

Being both Indigenous and white meant she wasn't fully accepted in either community. To complicate things further, her Indigenous status was questioned. According to Canadian law at that time, she was part of the Mohawk tribe because of her father. But Mohawk tradition dictates that children are born into their mother's family; as such, E. Pauline was not considered to be a Mohawk by her own tribe. Her father still encouraged her to learn about their Indigenous Canadian heritage. She was able to understand the Mohawk language but could not speak it. Her mixed heritage and search for identity would greatly influence her work. She used her mixed heritage to her advantage onstage; in fact, some scholars today have criticized her for appealing too much to white audiences. At the same time, her performances and art were centered on celebrating and defending her Indigenous perspective.

The youngest of four children, she was a sickly child, so she did not regularly attend the reservation school like her siblings. She spent her early life being educated at home on the reservation, taught by her mother, family members, and white governesses. At age fourteen she went to a local public high school, Brantford Central Collegiate, for a couple of years. An early and active reader, she spent a great deal of time reading from her family's large library. Her favorite authors included Lord Byron, Alfred Lord Tennyson, John Keats, Robert Browning, John Milton, and William Shakespeare. She also enjoyed reading works about Indigenous people, such as Henry Wadsworth Longfellow's *The Song of Hiawatha* and John Richardson's *Wacousta*. But her most favorite stories were those told by her paternal grandfather, who practiced Indigenous storytelling traditions. It was from his oral performances that she gained a flair for the performing and dramatic arts.

Rounding out her education, E. Pauline learned manners and poise, mainly from her mother. Her father worked as an interpreter for Mohawk, British, and Canadian officials. This meant that E. Pauline was often surrounded by notable figures, including royalty like Princess Louise Margaret of Prussia and Prince Arthur (son of Queen Victoria of England) and inventors like Alexander Graham Bell. She was taught to carry herself with "aloof dignity." The elegant manners and aristocratic air she learned would come in handy as she took to the stage as a young adult.

She also had a great memory and a gift for writing and reciting poetry. In 1892 she was invited to perform at an event hosted by the Young Men's Liberal Club of Toronto. She was the only girl. In a throaty, musical voice she recited one of her poems titled "A Cry from an Indian Wife." Her last verse read: "Go forth, nor bend to greed of white men's hands, / By right, by birth we Indians own these lands, / Though starved, crushed, plundered, lies our nation low . . . / Perhaps the white man's God has willed it so." After she read, there was a moment of complete silence followed by wild applause. She received the only encore of the evening and was lauded in the local newspapers. A reviewer in the *Toronto Globe* wrote, "Miss E. Pauline Johnson's may be said to have been the pleasantest contribution of the evening. It was like the voice of the nations that once possessed this country, who have wasted away before our civilization, speaking through this cultured, gifted, soft-faced descendant." Her success that night led to more invitations. She became Canada's first performance artist, touring all across the nation. In her early twenties she turned this gift into a way to make money, which she and her family needed when her father died in 1884.

She knew how to command an audience and learned from the popular Buffalo Bill shows, in which crowds watched reenactments of Wild West battles. In a letter to a notable poetry editor she wrote, "I am going to make a feature of costuming for recitals." She created a persona for her recitals, embracing her biracial identity. For the first half of her performance she went by her Mohawk name, Tekahionwake, which means "double life." She designed a costume based on a section of Longfellow's *The Song of Hiawatha* titled "The Death of Minnehaha." For the second half she wore an English evening gown with silk stockings and heels.

Some modern-day Indigenous scholars have criticized her for appealing to white audiences. But E. Pauline was making noise at a time when Indigenous women were silenced. Her work drew from both sides of her heritage. She was one of the first writers to explore the theme of the search for identity of those with mixed ancestry and to focus on issues affecting Native Americans. She wrote ballads about Indigenous history and presented images of Indigenous people being noble and brave. She wrote about racism, poverty, and violence. She wrote critically about prevailing stereotypes. She criticized racist portrayals of Indigenous people, describing them as "ignorant" and "dwarfed, erroneous, and delusive."

She was a successful working female artist. She toured for over seventeen years and became an international hit in Great Britain, Canada, and the United States. She performed on many stages, reading aloud various works. A prolific reader and writer, she wrote books and published many articles in various magazines and newspapers—all of which helped make Canada more well known on the international literary stage. Of her book *Legends of Vancouver*, she said, "The reviews have been magnificent, all the papers seem to think that I have done great things for the city by unearthing its surrounding romance."

Between her writing and her reciting, she was able to support herself and her family. This was a rare feat for a woman during this time. She persevered despite the obstacles she faced on the basis of her race, gender, and lack of formal education. In addition, unlike other performers of her day, she did not have a committed patron who funded her art. She had to rely on the income she received from her events. In this way and others, she defied conventions of the time and made a name for herself by doing what she loved best: reading, writing, and performing.

CHIEN-SHIUNG BREAKS BARRIERS

CHIEN-SHIUNG WU (1912–1997)

"I sincerely doubt that any open-minded person really believes in the faulty notion that women have no intellectual capacity for science and technology."

Chien-Shiung Wu was known as the "First Lady of Physics" and the "Queen of Nuclear Research." A Chinese American physicist, Chien-Shiung made significant contributions to science. She is most famous for working on the Manhattan Project, a top-secret research project that led to the creation of the first nuclear weapons, which were used in World War II. The Manhattan Project interviewers questioned her all day without revealing their mission. Chien-Shiung said, "I'm sorry, but if you wanted me not to know what you're doing, you should have cleaned the blackboards." She was able to figure out their top-secret work by reading their math calculations. She was hired on the spot.

Chien-Shiung is also famous for the "Wu experiment," which was named after her. She proved that identical nuclear particles do not always act alike and that the laws of nature are not entirely symmetrical. This experiment shattered our understanding of the physical world. Chien-Shiung took on a problem that other scientists were too scared to tackle. (Her name in Chinese befittingly means "courageous hero.") Not one to turn away from challenges, she said, "It is the courage to doubt that has long been established and the incessant search for its verification and proof that pushes the wheel of science forward."

To conduct the Wu experiment, she commuted between her university teaching job in New York and the laboratory in Washington, D.C. Her work was essential to proving the theory of two male physicists who ended up winning the Nobel Prize in Physics. Her experiment provided the "solution to the number-one riddle of atomic and nuclear physics."

Despite her sacrifices and her sound research, she was nevertheless passed over for a Nobel Prize and her work went unacknowledged. Fighting against sexism in science, she said, "I wonder whether the tiny atoms and nuclei, or the mathematical symbols, or the DNA molecules have any preference for either masculine or feminine treatment." To Chien-Shiung, actual math and science were not sexist; it was the fields of math and science that were incredibly sexist.

Chien-Shiung faced more sexism as a scientist in the United States than she did in China, where she grew up and studied with many female physicists as mentors. "It is shameful that there are so few women in science," she said. "In China, there are many, many women in physics. There is a misconception in America that women scientists are all dowdy spinsters. This is the fault of men. In Chinese society, a woman is valued for what she is, and men encourage her to accomplishments, yet she remains eternally feminine." Chien-Shiung didn't believe in compromising her gender for her professional goals. She believed women could have it all and fought against societal limitations. She also believed women and men should equally share household and childcare duties: "There is only one thing worse than coming home from the lab to a sink full of dirty dishes, and that is not going to the lab at all." Her only child, Vincent Yuan, would grow up to be a physicist just like his mother. He said, "She took care of me, but she needed to do her work. . . . Her work was her life and her fun."

Chien-Shiung's love of science started with her love of books and her family's commitment to education. Born in a village near Shanghai, China, she was one of three children, the only girl. Her mother was a teacher, and her father was an engineer. As progressives, her parents both valued education and supported women's rights. They encouraged Chien-Shiung, whose nickname was "Wei-Wei," to read from a young age. She started her early education by reciting poems and reading Chinese characters.

Chien-Shiung and her father were extremely close. He greatly influenced her reading habits. Before she could read herself, he read her the science articles from the Shanghai newspaper. He created an environment in which she was surrounded by books, magazines, and newspapers. A thoughtful child, Chien-Shiung did not often play outside with other children. Instead, she listened to the radio with her father. She loved keeping up with the news and asked a lot of questions. In many ways her father nurtured Chien-Shiung's natural curiosity. He was known to have modernized their small town. He created one of the first schools in China to admit girls and recruited female students from rich and poor families. As such, Chien-Shiung was educated at his school. She enjoyed reading poetry and Chinese classics such as *The Analects of Confucius*, a collection of sayings and ideas attributed to Confucius. She shared many of her father's reading interests, such as Western literature on democracy.

When she was ten, Chien-Shiung left her hometown to attend a boarding school to train to be a teacher, which was a respectable and popular career path for women at that time. It was there that she developed a serious passion for math, physics, and chemistry. Over summer breaks her father homeschooled her in science and math. Chien-Shiung spent hours poring over the textbooks he bought her, developing a lifelong habit of self-study. As a reader and a scientist, she was meticulous, detail-oriented, and precise. Known for being a perfectionist, she also loved being right. A student of hers commented, "She had a very, very strong sense that things had to be done right. If it was done sloppily, it wasn't worth doing because the results weren't reliable."

When she returned to her boarding school, she continued to self-study. During the day she learned about teaching. At night she borrowed science and math textbooks from classmates and studied on her own. She was accepted to China's most prestigious university, where, inspired by Marie Curie, she studied physics and graduated with top honors in 1934.

A female mentor encouraged Chien-Shiung to study in the United States, as she herself had done. At the time China did not offer advanced degree programs in atomic physics. So in 1936 Chien-Shiung boarded a ship to the United States, and unbeknownst to her, she would never see her parents again—they passed away before she was able to return to China. Originally, she was supposed to attend the University of Michigan, but she changed her mind when she found out women were not allowed to enter through the front door of the student union. She transferred schools, completing her doctorate at the University of California, Berkeley.

Barred from research positions because of gender discrimination, Chieng-Shiung accepted a teaching job at Smith College. During World War II males were sent abroad to fight, which opened up job opportunities for women to fill in the labor gaps. Due to a shortage of male professors, Chien-Shiung was eventually able to secure a research position at Princeton University, then Columbia University. As her research and reputation grew, she became the leading expert in her field of physics, winning many awards and accolades. She was the first recipient of the Wolf Prize in Physics (1978), which honors scientists overlooked for the Nobel Prize. She is among the world's most distinguished female experimental physicists.

She was often the only woman and/or Asian American in the room. She was advised by her father to "ignore the obstacles" and "put your head down and keep walking forward." Her persistence and passion helped her overcome discrimination and break down barriers. Her avid reading in math and science gave her the confidence to succeed in fields dominated by men. Because of her, more and more women were taken seriously in the science fields and recognized for their contributions. Her only grandchild, Jada Yuan, said, "She was fighting to be seen and respected at a time when women and Chinese people in America rarely were."

After retiring, Chien-Shiung committed herself to promoting women in science, technology, engineering, and math. To this day, her 1966 book *Beta Decay* is still a standard reference for nuclear physicists, widely read and cited around the world. Chien-Shiung grew up reading science textbooks, so it seems appropriate for this seminal textbook to be part of her legacy.

INDIRA LEARNS FROM LETTERS

INDIRA GANDHI (1917–1984)

"And one of the biggest responsibilities of the educated women today
is how to synthesize what has been valuable and timeless in our ancient traditions
with what is good and valuable in modern thought."

Indira Nehru Gandhi is a powerhouse in the annals of world history, having served four terms as India's first female prime minister. But when she was born, an only child, her family hoped for a boy. Her disappointed grandmother announced that "it" had been born. Her grandfather was not of the same mind. He said, "For all we know, [Indira] may prove better than a thousand sons." Indira loved her grandfather, who encouraged her to have a sense of Indian pride. Her grandfather also had one of the finest private libraries in India. She could often be found reading there or sitting alone in trees reading fairy tales, folktales from Rajasthan, religious Hindu stories, Lewis Carroll's *Alice in Wonderland*, F. W. Bain's *A Digit of the Moon*, and more. She loved fantasies, adventures, and nature. "From childhood," she said, "I looked upon trees as life giving and a refuge. I loved climbing and hiding there, in a little place which was my own."

Even though Indira was not the boy the family wanted, she was treated like a princess; in fact, she was a political princess. Her father was Jawaharlal Nehru, India's first prime minister after India won independence from Great Britain. Indira became an adviser to her father and then followed in his footsteps.

Indira grew up in a rich, aristocratic family and wanted for nothing. Yet she had an unhappy and lonely childhood. Her parents had an arranged marriage, as was the custom of the time. Her mother, Kamala, was often ignored by the family. Of her mother, Indira said,

"She had no formal education; her mind had not gone through the educational process." Indira vowed to be educated and became a huge advocate of educating girls: "Women's education is almost more important that the education of boys and men," she believed.

Kamala spent most of her time alone in her room, sickly and often bedridden. Indira would keep her company, listening to her stories. She learned the Hindi language and her family's Indian history from her. Kamala eventually died of tuberculosis. Between taking care of her mother from a young age and being on the road a lot supporting her father's political campaigns, Indira had an uncommon childhood. "I had this tremendous feeling of responsibility," she said. "I felt I was looking after myself, and whether I was or wasn't, I thought I was looking after my parents." Additionally, Indira's education was inconsistent. She attended schools in India, Switzerland, and England. And there were times when she didn't go to school at all. She was mostly taught at home by tutors and learned how to read quickly. She had to take her college entrance exams twice, having failed Latin.

Although she wasn't always a strong student, Indira was an avid reader. She especially enjoyed biographies and political histories of independence movements and rebellions. Books filled her empty hours and expanded her understanding of the world. Her father was a huge influence on her reading habits. "What I wanted to read at that young age were fairy tales," she explained. "I had to either read them in the bathroom or with a blanket over my head. My father disapproved strongly. He wanted me to read H. G. Wells. There were many words I didn't understand, many concepts I didn't understand. But he said, 'It doesn't matter. You must read.' So, I read. And a long time afterwards, without re-reading it, I understood what it was about."

Jawaharlal was often away on business or jailed for his political convictions. So he and Indira had limited contact when she was young. He supplemented Indira's learning with letters—they exchanged hundreds over several decades. They shared their thoughts, experiences, and opinions about books. In an exchange from 1932, they discussed more than sixty books. Jawaharlal recommended titles about nature and natural history, gifting her with several books of this kind with handwritten inscriptions inside. Indira said, "My father's letters had explained how rocks, stones, and trees told not only their own story but those of the people and creatures who lived amongst them. Very early I became a conservationist with a strong feeling of companionship and kinship with all living things." In a 1940 letter, she wrote to him, "I have been reading, in the *Reader's Digest*, a condensation from the book *Flowering Earth* by D. C. Peattie. I am sure it would fascinate you, as it did me." This was one of the few books Indira recommended to her father.

Among her father's papers, there was an invitation to a "Book Tea" that he hosted to celebrate his sixty-fourth birthday. In it, he instructed his guests: "You should represent a well-known book in English, Hindu, or Urdu, or any other book of international reputation. You will be required to guess the names of books represented by others. The highbrows who make the largest number of correct guesses will be installed in seats of honour and presented with souvenirs of the occasion." Along with tea, sherbet, ice cream, and lemonade were offered. But books were the main theme of the party. Growing up in a family that celebrated books, it is no wonder that Indira was an avid reader.

In 1942 Indira married Feroze Gandhi, an Indian freedom fighter and journalist. Their marriage lasted almost twenty years until he died of a heart attack. Neither Indira nor Feroze was related to Mahatma Gandhi, yet Mahatma influenced both of them. After joining Mahatma's independence movement, Feroze changed his last name from "Ghandy" to "Gandhi" as a tribute to his hero. Feroze and Indira both saw Mahatma as a mentor.

Indira had met Mahatma when she was five years old and referred to him as her "uncle." Growing up, she was surrounded by the politics of her father and of Mahatma. She had been preparing for a political career since youth. She believed in an independent and self-sufficient India and wanted to serve her country. She was the first woman to be elected to lead a country. She said, "The responsibility to look after national interest is on the shoulder of every citizen of India. . . . I have lived a long life and I am proud that I spend the whole of my life in the service of my people. I am only proud of this and nothing else. I shall continue to serve until my last breath and when I die, I can say, that every drop of my blood will invigorate India and strengthen it."

As India's prime minister, she centralized power and turned India into the sole regional power of South Asia. She cultivated an international presence that helped establish India as an emerging global power. In addition, her love for nature, which she gained from reading, spilled over into her political career. As a naturalist, Indira supported India's best-known wildlife conservation program, Project Tiger. She also protected other endangered species and supported laws that preserved wildlife and forests.

Books continued to influence Indira's politics throughout her life and career. From a young age, she was inspired by Joan of Arc, a martyr, saint, and military leader who led the French army to victory over the English during the Hundred Years' War. She said, "She was one of the first people I read about with enthusiasm." She even told her aunt once, "Someday, I am going to lead my people to freedom just as Joan of Arc did."

SHIRLEY BLAZES TRAILS

SHIRLEY CHISHOLM (1924–2005)

"The next time a woman runs, or a black, a Jew or anyone from a group that the country is 'not ready' to elect to its highest office, I believe he or she will be taken seriously from the start. The door is not open yet, but it is ajar."

Shirley Chisholm was used to blazing trails. She wasn't afraid to be first. She was the first Black woman elected to the U.S. Congress. She was the first Black woman to serve on the House Rules Committee. She was also the first woman and first Black American to run for president from a major political party. She said, "I ran because someone had to do it first. In this country, everybody is supposed to be able to run for President, but that's never been really true. I ran because most people think the country is not ready for a black candidate, not ready for a woman candidate."

But Shirley wanted to change all that. "I ran for the presidency, despite hopeless odds, to demonstrate the sheer will and refusal to accept the status quo . . . to give a voice to the people the major candidates were ignoring." She asserted her constitutional right to do so. She stayed in the race for as long as she could. Her supporters followed her on the "Chisholm Trail." In doing so, she paved the way for others. Presidential candidates from marginalized communities after her lauded Chisholm as an inspiration, including Barack Obama, Hillary Clinton, and Kamala Harris. Coincidentally, Kamala launched her presidential campaign forty-seven years after Chisholm's campaign. The key to Shirley's success was to "reject not only the stereotypes that others hold of us, but also the stereotypes that we hold of ourselves."

Born in Brooklyn to immigrant parents from the West Indies (her father was originally from Guyana), she was the oldest of four daughters. She exhibited leadership skills as early as two and a half years old. In her own words, "I was already dominating other children around me—with my mouth. I lectured and ordered them around." During the Great Depression of the 1930s, times were tough for Shirley's parents, who were not making enough money to feed their growing family. So Shirley and her sisters were sent to live on her grandparents' farm in Barbados for seven years. Although Shirley was sad to be separated from her parents, she thrived in Barbados, recalling, "Granny gave me strength, dignity, and love. I learned from an early age that I was somebody." Everyone on Barbados was brown like her, so she had many role models of Black folks being in charge. She set on a course to ensure that others saw her as a role model as well.

Shirley attended a one-room schoolhouse in Barbados that served over a hundred students, aged four to eleven. She received what she called a "strict, traditional" British education since Barbados was a British colony at the time. She said, "If I speak and write easily now, that early education is the main reason." A quick learner, she could read and write before she was five years old. She stayed up late at night reading books by the light of a kerosene lamp. She would often read a book a night.

She returned to Brooklyn as a teenager and attended an all-girls integrated high school. To no one's surprise, she excelled in reading, writing, and debating. But she struggled with U.S. history because she'd learned British history in Barbados. To her dismay, she was placed in a lower grade. She received tutoring, read more books, and got caught up. Whenever there were people or topics that interested her, she would go to the library and read all the books she could find about them. She ended up loving U.S. history, especially the history of women in politics.

From her time in Barbados, Shirley developed a slight British accent, for which she was bullied. She ignored the teasing and escaped into reading. She would read about ten books a month. During her free time she volunteered at hospitals reading to senior citizens.

Shirley's father, Charles St. Hill, influenced her greatly. Shirley's family ate dinner together every night. Charles wanted his children to tell him what they'd learned in school. Formally, he had a fifth-grade education, but he self-educated by reading and was very knowledgeable. He advised his daughters, "Study and make something of yourselves. . . . God gave you a brain; use it." He read every evening, sometimes falling asleep over his book. Reading was a mandatory chore in Charles's house. Shirley said, "Papa read everything within reach. If he saw a man passing out handbills, he would cross the street to get one and read it." Charles bought two or three newspapers a day. Growing up, Shirley was exposed to political readings and conversations. For example, her father introduced her to the work of Marcus Garvey, a Black nationalist leader from Jamaica.

Everyone in the family had library cards. They went to the library every Saturday. They checked out three books each, the most they could check out at a time. Shirley said, "Each of us had a dictionary, and our Christmas presents were books, often one of those endless 'adventure' series such as the Nancy Drew or Bobbsey Twins stories."

Shirley's reading topics drastically changed when she went to Brooklyn College. She joined the Harriet Tubman Society, an all-Black student group that discussed current events and studied the ideas of prominent Black figures. She said, "There I first heard people other than my father talk about white oppression, black racial consciousness, and black pride." She found herself spending hours in the college library and became known as a "book-worm," choosing to read rather than party. She dived into learning about her heritage. She read books about Black American heroes such as Harriet Tubman, Frederick Douglas, W. E. B. Dubois, and George W. Carver. She also learned about African history and literature.

Reading made her more aware of the racial inequities around her. Because of that awareness, she dedicated her life to creating a more just society. Shirley never took "no" for an answer: "I have no intention of just sitting quietly and observing. I intend to focus attention on the nation's problems." Thus she became known as "Fighting Shirley" and introduced more than fifty laws during her time in Congress. She fought for racial and gender equity. She fought for economic justice to support low-income communities. She fought to end the Vietnam War. "I am the people's politician," she declared. She also famously said, "If they don't give you a seat at the table, bring a folding chair."

PATSY PUSHES BACK

PATSY MINK (1927–2002)

*"The pursuit of Title IX and its enforcement has been
a personal crusade for me. Equal educational opportunities for women and
girls is essential for us to achieve parity in all aspects of our society."*

Patsy Takemoto Mink was a political pioneer. She is most famous for championing Title IX, legislation aimed at ending gender discrimination in higher education. Title IX lifted barriers for women in sports and opened doors for women to attend colleges and universities—issues near and dear to Patsy's own life. "I consider Title IX to be one of my most significant accomplishments as a Member of Congress," she said. "Since its enactment, Title IX has opened the doors of educational opportunity to literally millions of girls and women across the country. Title IX has helped to tear down inequitable admissions policies, increase opportunities for women in nontraditional fields of study such as math and science, improve vocational educational opportunities for women, reduce discrimination against pregnant students and teen mothers, protect female students from sexual harassment in our schools, and increase athletic opportunities for girls and women." After her death Title IX was renamed the Patsy T. Mink Equal Opportunity in Education Act.

Born in Hawai'i, Patsy grew up among the sugarcane business. Her grandparents were recruited from Japan to work in the sugarcane fields. Her father, one of the first Japanese American civil engineering graduates from the University of Hawai'i, was a land surveyor for sugar plantations. Because of her father's professional job, Patsy enjoyed a comfortable life compared to other Japanese Americans in her community, who lived in the plantation camps. She was raised on two acres with pigs, chickens, rabbits, and turkeys. She spent time exploring the nearby mountains picking mushrooms and bamboo shoots. She was also a Girl Scout and took piano and hula lessons.

Even though she was taught to sew and cook, Patsy was also encouraged to play sports with her brother and male cousins. She loved football and baseball. She described herself as a "pushy little sister." She recalled that she and her brother were always treated equally in their household: "[Our parents] never said that I couldn't ride a bike. In fact, when my brother got one, the only difference was that since he was a year older he got his a year ahead."

Despite her idyllic family life, Patsy was not shielded from inequality. She saw firsthand how white bosses unfairly treated Asian and Native Hawaiian workers. She saw how differently people were treated because of their skin color or heritage. She realized that laws could be unfair. At an early age Patsy was exposed to politics. She remembered going to election rallies and sitting on grass-cloth mats, listening to Hawaiian music and endless speeches. She realized that "politics was an important thing, that being a citizen was important." These rallies may have sparked her interest in politics, but at that time she was more fascinated with the field of medicine after undergoing surgery for appendicitis. She said, "From the time I was four, I thought I was going to be a doctor, and some may have laughed, but nobody ever said, 'You can't be a doctor.'"

Also at age four she insisted on starting school early. With special permission from the principal, she began attending the local school with her older brother. She was thrilled to be surrounded by books, teachers, and more playmates who looked like her. Because of her father's job, Patsy and her brother had learned to speak English at home. Because of their English proficiency, they were transferred to an English Standard School when Patsy was in the fourth grade. Instead of being with other Asian Americans and Native Hawaiians, Patsy was now going to a school filled with white kids and white teachers. Although she did well, she described the school as "intimidating and unfriendly." She often felt "unrecognized for her accomplishments."

She had to take a train and a bus to get there, which meant few classmates lived nearby. She didn't have many friends and was lonely. She turned to books and the radio for companionship. She discovered the power of words. She was a devoted listener of President

Franklin D. Roosevelt's fireside chats. She also spent hours reading books out loud while perched in a tree. She would perform the words of each character. Her favorite books were about inspirational leaders. For example, she loved reading about Mahatma Gandhi and was impressed by his ideas about nonviolent resistance.

When Patsy turned fourteen, Pearl Harbor was attacked, which marked U.S. entry into World War II. "We didn't know what was happening," she said. "The Boy Scouts came and told us to turn out our lights. . . . We might be considered 'Jap spies.'" She experienced the injustice of Japanese incarceration in which Japanese Americans were forcefully removed from their homes and held in various incarceration camps that were spread out across the nation, west of the Mississippi River. Her father, whose only crime was being of Japanese descent, was accused of being disloyal and taken away for questioning. Luckily, he was not incarcerated like other Japanese Americans were. (The U.S. government incarcerated about 2,270 Japanese Americans in Hawai'i. In total, about 120,000 Japanese Americans were incarcerated.) To avoid suspicion, Patsy's family lived in a small room in their house "lit by one light" after sunset. Patsy remembered being called a "dirty Jap" in school. Despite this, she volunteered at the Red Cross, knitting scarves and rolling bandages to support the war effort.

She persevered and continued with her schoolwork. She studied hard and graduated top of her class. In her senior year she was elected as the first female class president at her high school. She said, "Like most of the decisions I've made in politics, it seemed like a good idea at that time. Why not? The football team backed me. That's why I won."

With dreams of becoming a doctor, Patsy began her college career at the University of Hawai'i at Mānoa, where she participated on the varsity debate team and was elected president of her pre-medical students' club. She then decided to continue her education on the mainland, attending the University of Nebraska. But she found the university to be "polluted with germs, germs of a discriminating nature." She learned that "the dormitories were not open for people like myself." She also learned that "affiliation with sororities and fraternities was impossible for anyone with skin any darker than the superciliously arrogant whites." Patsy thought these policies were unfair. She read about other protests. She gave speeches and wrote letters to campus leaders and local newspapers. She won her fight to effect change, forcing the university to update its policies. Despite her victory and being elected president of the Unaffiliated Students of the University of Nebraska, she returned to Hawai'i to finish her degree when a medical condition required surgery.

Through it all, it became obvious that Patsy was good at politics, but she was still committed to being a doctor. She thought her leadership positions so far would be good for her medical school applications, but even with good grades and extracurriculars, no medical school admitted her because she was a girl and a person of color. So Patsy switched gears and set her sights on becoming a lawyer, and she was admitted as one of only two women at the University of Chicago's law school. But after graduation no law firm would hire her either—again because she was a woman and a person of color. Determined to achieve her goal, Patsy started her own law firm, becoming the first Japanese American woman to practice law in her home state of Hawai'i.

Patsy wanted to do something about the discrimination she had faced. The arena for that was politics. "I didn't start off wanting to be in politics," she admitted. "Not being able to get a job from anybody changed things." She wanted to amend laws and policies that discriminated against women and people of color. She used all that she learned from reading about effective leaders. She said, "I faced overwhelming odds: I was not from a political family, and I had no visible support in the community, no organizational support." She learned about the election process and about leadership from reading and from doing.

In addition to being a woman of color, she was not a party favorite and was underfunded. She ran for several offices in Hawai'i and lost. But she kept trying, running for local, state, and national positions. Her first elected position was in the Hawaiian Territorial Legislature (before Hawai'i became a state). She eventually became the first woman of color elected to the U.S. House of Representatives and the first Asian American woman to serve in Congress. She was also the first Asian American to run for president in the United States. She didn't get many votes and was called "Patsy Pink" for her opposition to the Vietnam War. None of this stopped her from fighting for equality. Known for having a distinct, forthright manner and for having her own mind, she became a champion for women, children, and the impoverished. Of Patsy, a University of Hawai'i law professor said, "If she saw something that was wrong, she was going to push until it was corrected."

PATSY MINK

Once Patsy learned to win, she couldn't stop winning. Not even death stopped her. In August 2002 she was hospitalized for pneumonia and died a month later. But at the time she was running for office, so her name was still on the ballot. She won by a landslide, post-mortem. As she said, "All I ever wanted to do is to help work for a better community and to fight for the preservation of life, liberty, and happiness for ourselves and for our children."

AUDRE REFUSES TO BE SILENT
AUDRE LORDE (1934–1992)

"When we speak, we are afraid our words will not be heard nor welcomed,
but when we are silent, we are still afraid, so it is better to speak."

Audre Lorde, an internationally recognized activist and author, chose her own name. Born Audrey, she dropped the *y* from her first name, preferring the artistic symmetry of having both her first and last names ending with the letter *e*. In her final years, while she battled cancer, she renamed herself yet again as Gamba Adisa, an African name meaning "she who makes her meaning known."

Audre was her own person. She was fearless, living by her own rules. She was loud and proud about all of her identities, describing herself as "black, lesbian, mother, warrior, poet." She said, "If I didn't define myself for myself, I would be crunched into other people's fantasies for me and eaten alive." She dedicated her life to liberating herself and others, fighting against racism, sexism, classism, and homophobia. She focused on marginalized communities who get left out of movements, like the women of color who were not fully represented in the fight for women's rights. Audre empowered others to find their voices.

But it took a while for Audre to find her own voice. Born in Harlem to immigrant parents from the Caribbean, she faced adversity from an early age. Her mother, who was of mixed ancestry, was very critical of Audre's dark skin, which she inherited from her father, who was from Barbados. There was much tension between mother and daughter at home. At school Audre faced other issues. She was bigger than other children her age, she was legally blind, and she didn't talk for the first few years of her life—all of which gave cause for bullying.

At age four Audre learned to read and write. But she couldn't read numbers yet, so she was often silent in school. "I was ashamed of not being able to read my numbers," she said, "so when my turn came to read I couldn't, because I didn't have the right place." She befriended a fellow outcast, Alvin, who couldn't read but who knew his numbers. As a team, they worked out their "own system": Audre read the words and Alvin read the numbers.

Audre learned to talk at the same time she learned to read. She discovered a deep love for poems. Reading and writing poetry gave Audre her voice. She saw life in terms of poetry. She saw poems everywhere and in everything. As she explained it, "Everything was like a poem, with different curves, different levels." She recalled starting with nursey rhymes. In the second or third grade she remembered reading in the children's room of her local library in Harlem. She picked up a book of poems illustrated by Arthur Rackham. She said, "These were old books, the library in Harlem used to get the oldest books, in the worst condition." In these old books she found new ways of thinking. She developed an acute sensitivity for the feel and sounds of words. She especially loved her mother's stories about life in the West Indies and saw poetry in those stories.

Once silent, Audre learned to speak in poems. She said, "I would read poems, and I would memorize them." When people asked her questions, she would respond by quoting poems: "I would recite a poem and somewhere in that poem would be a line or a feeling I would be sharing. In other words, I literally communicated through poetry." One of the first poems she memorized was Walter de la Mare's "The Listeners." Her favorite poets were Edna St. Vincent Millay, and John Keats.

She started writing poetry around twelve or thirteen years old and used it to express her thoughts and feelings. She saw her poems as a "duty to speak the truth as I see it." She refused to be silent any longer, stating, "There are so many silences to be broken." She encouraged others to raise their voice against oppression and injustice, warning them, "Your silence will not protect you."

She wrote about both joy and pain. She published her first poem while in high school. Originally, she had submitted the poem to her high school's literary journal, but the journal rejected the piece, which was about teen love, claiming it was inappropriate. Not to be deterred, Audre got it published in *Seventeen* magazine instead, reaching a much wider audience. While in high school she also participated in poetry workshops sponsored by the Harlem Writers Guild. However, she felt she was not accepted there because she was "both crazy and queer." Audre believed in being open about her sexuality and encouraged others to be out and proud as well. "In the past, I stayed home and stayed silent," she shared. "I believed that since I never had a public 'coming out' moment, it meant that I was not proud. However, this is not true. I am proud, and now, more than ever, it is important that I also be visible in an effort to unite as one voice to work together for a brighter future for everyone." She sought to find her own spaces and her own ways of doing things. She connected with others who saw themselves as outcasts. Audre often talked about the power of working together, using differences as strengths.

Audre noticed that her experiences as a Black, gay woman living in America weren't included in the stories she read in school. She said, "All our storybooks were about people who were very different from us. They were blond and white and lived in houses with trees around and had dogs named Spot. I didn't know people like that any more than I knew people like Cinderella who lived in castles. Nobody wrote stories about us." Failing to see herself in the stories she read would inspire Audre's life work, which was to tell her story and the stories of people like her.

Audre became a powerful voice for marginalized people. Among her many identities, she was an award-winning poet/writer, activist, librarian, and teacher. She is best known for her radical thinking, giving voice to issues of race, gender, and sexuality. Her work was personal and political and aimed to help folks survive various forms of oppression. Her most famous books include *Sister Outsider* and *Zami: A New Spelling of My Name*. Her ideas continue to shape conversations today. She said, "In our work and in our living, we must recognize that difference is a reason for celebration and growth, rather than a reason for destruction."

TEMPLE THINKS IN PICTURES

TEMPLE GRANDIN (1947–)

"The world needs different kinds of minds to work together."

Temple Grandin has a brilliant mind. She is famous for inventing tools and systems designed to humanely handle animals. Her inventions are used everywhere and have changed the way farmers treat and care for livestock. Because of her, the meat industry has been significantly revolutionized toward more humane meat production and animal-handling processes. Temple is a highly regarded scientist despite facing obstacles as a woman in a male-dominated field. She received a doctorate in science at a time when very few women were doing so. Underestimated her whole life, she is no stranger to struggle, nor is she a stranger to shattering limitations placed upon her.

She was born into a wealthy family, but her life was anything but easy. Even as a baby, she was unique in that she did not like to be touched. Temple did not know how to communicate her needs and wants. She said, "I can remember the frustration of not being able to talk. I knew what I wanted to say, but I could not get the words out, so I would just scream." She didn't talk until she was four years old. Instead, she screamed, peeped, and hummed. She had control issues that resulted in her breaking out into violent rages and impulsive behaviors. She had difficulty interacting with other people and was teased for having tics. She was also hypersensitive to stimuli and overwhelmed by smells. She described her ears as microphones, transmitting everything at loud volumes.

Doctors originally thought she had brain damage. But eventually, she was properly diagnosed with autism—a broad range of conditions characterized by challenges with social skills and communication. Temple grew up in a time when little was known about autism.

There were many prejudices against people who were "different." In the past people with autism were often sent away to hospitals or institutions. Fortunately, Temple had a champion in her mother, Eustacia Cutler. As an adult, Temple became her own champion and a champion of others, both humans and animals.

Temple is just one example of a person with autism. Although she has become a spokesperson for autism, she, like all people in general, is unique. She experiences autism in a different way from others, yet her message of respecting and valuing human differences applies to everyone. Because of advocates like Temple, the general public's knowledge and attitudes about autism have changed for the better. Temple works hard to destigmatize autism; she wants autism to be seen in a positive light and uses humor to do so. "What would happen if the autism gene was eliminated from the gene pool? You would have a bunch of people standing around in a cave, chatting and socializing and not getting anything done," she joked.

Eustacia made sure Temple got the best care and education, including speech therapists and private tutors. Temple credits her mother for instilling in her a love of books: "My mother really worked on fostering reading. She read to us, both my sister and I, when we were little kids and books were always a really important thing in our house." However, learning to read was a struggle for Temple at first. She said, "I had trouble learning to read originally. My mother had to teach me to read when I was in third grade and then once I learned how to read, I just took off."

Learning to read opened many worlds to Temple. A big fan of libraries, she said, "The only place on earth where immortality is provided is in libraries. This is the collective memory of humanity." Libraries are especially important for marginalized communities who may not have access to books. Temple said, "Libraries are just a lifeline for parents with autistic kids." Autistic people, like all people, deserve access to books. Libraries are places where people can go and learn more about their passions and interests. Temple is a testament to this—she read books to develop her love of science.

Temple has been vocal about how much she "loved books as a child." She loved reading about animals and inventors, so it's no surprise that she grew up to be an inventor and animal scientist. Her favorite books included *Black Beauty* by Anna Sewell, *The Wonderful Wizard of Oz* by L. Frank Baum, and a book about famous inventors. Inventors, she said, "were just so clever in figuring out how to make things. I remember reading about the sewing machine, and they had to stop the needle from snapping off, so they put the needle eye next to the point. And that kind of stuff fascinated me." Reading about innovations inspired her to do the same, spending hours tinkering.

Temple also read many Greek myths. She particularly enjoyed the story of Icarus, who flew too close to the sun and ended up drowning in the sea. She was not a fan of Shakespeare's plays, though. Of *Romeo and Juliet*, she said, "I never knew what they were up to." In general, she preferred reading about science and science fiction—and still does to this day. One of her favorite sci-fi characters is Data, a droid from *Star Trek*. (Data also loves animals and even wrote a poem to his cat Spot titled "Ode to Spot.")

Temple remains an avid reader. "I like reading novels. I don't really like mysteries because there's too much convoluted plot." She sometimes struggles to understand characters' motivations, complex storylines, figurative language, and humor. She doesn't like "flowery language." She said, "My interests are factual and my recreational reading consists mostly of science and livestock publications. I have little interest in novels with complicated interpersonal relationships, because I am unable to remember the sequence of events. Detailed descriptions of new technologies in science fiction or descriptions of exotic places are much more interesting."

As a photo-realistic visual thinker, she sees the world in pictures, not words. She thinks this is how animals see the world too. She creates a library of visual experiences in her head. Reading allows her to add to her mind's library. As she explains it, "I'm a visual thinker, not a language-based thinker. My mind works like Google for images. You put in a key word; it brings up pictures . . . language, for me, narrates the pictures in my mind." In regard to reading, "I like stuff that describes faraway, interesting places, and then as I read it I can, like, watch a movie in my mind, like maybe a science fiction book that describes another planet or describes a futuristic technology. And then I can see it."

In addition to books, Temple's love of science was inspired by her love of the outdoors. She believes playing outdoors as a child gave her a strong foundation in the sciences. Observing nature made her more curious and increased her sense of wonder, essential traits for a scientist. "I could sit on the beach for hours dribbling sand through my fingers and fashioning miniature mountains," she recalled. "Each particle of sand intrigued me as though I were a scientist looking through a microscope."

When Temple was fifteen, she spent a summer at her stepfather's sister's farm in Arizona. This experience changed her life. She learned she had a lot in common with animals. After observing the farm animals, she realized that she thinks like a cow because her emotions are simpler than most people's and she's always anxious. To help calm the animals, she invented a "squeeze machine" at age eighteen. She saw animal handlers leading animals into a tight space to get shots of medicine. Her invention uses gentle pressure caused by the tight space to ease the animals' anxiety. (Gentle pressure releases chemicals called "endorphins" that promote a sense of well-being.) She applied this concept to create a similar "hug machine" to help relieve some of her own stress.

Temple was born curious. She is much more than a person who has autism, as autism is only one part of human diversity. She said, "If I could snap my fingers and be nonautistic, I would not. Autism is part of what I am." That stated, she insists, "Autism's an important part of who I am, but I'm a college professor and an animal scientist first. And I wouldn't change 'cause I like the logical way I think." Temple is a well-known scientist and professor, the author of many books and articles, and a popular public speaker. In addition to changing the way people think about autism and neurodiversity, she has changed the way people think about animals and about women in science. She champions the idea of being "different, not less."

SALLY REACHES FOR THE STARS
SALLY RIDE (1951–2012)

"If it wasn't for the women's movement, I wouldn't be where I am today."

Dr. Sally Ride was the youngest American, the first American woman, and the first lesbian astronaut to fly in space. When Sally launched into space, feminist Gloria Steinem said, "Millions of little girls are going to sit by their television sets and see they can be astronauts, heroes, explorers, and scientists."

Sally's first word was "no." She knew what she wanted and, more importantly, what she didn't want. Sally's younger sister, Karen, known as "Bear," said she loved to be in control and always had to win. At two years old Sally couldn't pronounce her name correctly, so she called herself "Sassy." To those who knew her, this made total sense—Sally was definitely sassy. She was independent and headstrong from the start.

Sally's parents were both teachers, so their house was filled with books. Sally was an avid reader her entire life. She read everything she could get her hands on and couldn't pass up a bookstore. As an adult, she visited bookstores in many countries around the world. She could be found in the science section, mystery section, and the children's section. Sally was curious and loved to learn new things. She said, "Studying whether there's life on Mars or studying how the universe began, there's something magical about pushing back the frontiers of knowledge. That's something that is almost part of being human and I'm certain that will continue."

Sally always loved being outdoors. She was a gifted athlete who ran on her toes. She played baseball and other sports with the boys in her neighborhood. But she did not like being called a tomboy. She said, "Tomboy, when applied to a girl, means a girl acting like a boy. As opposed to a girl acting like a girl."

Newspapers were an important part of Sally's reading history. By age five she'd learned to read by consuming and laughing at the comics. She would race her father every morning to get the newspaper. She devoured the sports pages and memorized baseball statistics. She was hooked on math—she loved figuring out the logic and seeing patterns in the numbers. At age nine Sally and her family toured Europe for a year. She had many adventures, but her favorite moments were getting letters from her grandparents, who would send her newspaper clippings from the sports pages.

Upon returning to the United States, Sally was a whole year ahead in school. She was able to skip a grade in elementary school and supplemented her education by reading a lot of books. Her favorites included the Nancy Drew series about a girl detective, the Danny Dunn adventure series about a boy who wants to be a scientist, and the James Bond spy novels. She also loved reading science fiction and the short stories of newswriter Damon Runyon. Of course, she also loved reading about science. She had her own subscription to *Scientific American*, which she read from cover to cover. She enjoyed completing the brainteasers. Like many kids at that time, she also read *Mad*, a humor magazine that first launched as a comic book series.

Sally went to an all-girls high school and benefited greatly from it. She said, "I didn't succumb to the stereotypes that science wasn't for girls. I got encouragement from my parents. I never ran into a teacher or a counselor who told me that science was for boys." She had several male and female mentors who inspired her to pursue science. Her favorite was Dr. Elizabeth Mommaerts, a science teacher Sally described as "logic personified." She challenged Sally to "be curious, ask questions, and think for myself."

In 1977 Sally was finishing her doctorate at Stanford University. One morning she was eating breakfast in the cafeteria. As was her habit from a young age, she was reading the newspaper. She saw an advertisement from the National Aeronautics and Space Administration (NASA), which was recruiting new astronauts. For the first time NASA was allowing women to apply. Sally said, "The moment I saw that ad, I knew that's what I wanted to do." She applied that day and soon learned that she was destined to soar into space.

In space Sally had the best seat in the world. "I remember unstrapping from my seat, floating over to the window, and that's when I got my first view of Earth. Just a spectacular view, and a chance to see our planet as a planet. I could see coral reefs off the coast of Australia. A huge storm swirling in the ocean. I could see an enormous dust storm building over northern Africa . . . just unbelievable sights."

Sally died in 2012 from pancreatic cancer. A private person, she kept her sickness and her love life out of the public eye. Her sister, Bear, said, "Most people did not know that Sally had a wonderfully loving relationship with [Dr.] Tam O'Shaughnessy for 27 years. Sally never hid her relationship with Tam. . . . Sally's very close friends, of course, knew of their love for each other." With Bear's statement issued after Sally died, Sally was acknowledged as the first lesbian in space, and in 2014 she was inducted into the Legacy Walk, an outdoor public display in Chicago that celebrates LGBTQ+ history and people.

In addition to being life partners, Sally and Tam were also business partners committed to helping women and girls pursue science, technology, engineering, and mathematics (STEM). Sally and Tam started the Sally Ride Science company in 2001 to "make science and engineering cool again." Together they wrote a series of children's books that explore space and investigate the impacts of climate change. They also provided training for teachers and programs to give young people hands-on experience with science. Family and friends indicated that Sally's main concern in her last days was making sure that Sally Ride Science survived her passing. Today Sally Ride Science is managed by the University of California, San Diego, and Tam continues to serve in a leadership role.

Of her sister, Bear said, "Sally lived her life to the fullest with boundless energy, curiosity, intelligence, passion, joy, and love. . . . Sally died the same way she lived: without fear. Sally's signature statement was 'Reach for the Stars.' Surely, she did this, and blazed a trail for all the rest of us." As an astronaut and scientist, Sally was a role model for girls everywhere. For Sally, there were no limits to a girl's ambitions. Sally said, "I would like to be remembered as someone who was not afraid to do what she wanted to do, and as someone who took risks along the way in order to achieve her goals."

OPRAH INFLUENCES AMERICA

OPRAH WINFREY (1954–)

"When you educate a woman, you set her free. Had I not had books and education in Mississippi, I would have believed that's all there was."

Oprah Winfrey is perhaps the most important reader of our time. She founded Oprah's Book Club—when launched, it was the most popular book club ever. She is one of the few Black and few female billionaires in North America. She is also very generous with her money, having donated millions to support various causes. She is the first African American woman to own her own production company. She is an author who also started her own magazine and TV channel. She is an award-winning actress and former host of *The Oprah Winfrey Show*, which was the highest-rated TV program of its kind. Her show reached over fifteen million people daily.

Before Oprah became a household name, she was a poor girl living in central Mississippi. She said, "I wouldn't take anything for having been raised the way that I was. . . . It is because I was raised poor, and no running water, and going to the well, and getting whippings that I have such compassion for people who have experienced it . . . it has given me a broader understanding and a deeper appreciation for every little and big thing that I now have." She grew up on her grandparents' farm in an old house without electricity or indoor plumbing. She was often alone, as no other children lived nearby. Her only toy was a doll made from a corncob. A lover of stories, she would tell tales to the farm animals, her main companions.

Oprah's grandmother, who had only a third-grade education, used the Bible to teach Oprah the shape of letters. From her grandmother, Oprah learned that words have meanings.

"My grandmother, who was very harsh, but like a lot of Black parents during that era—the idea of hugging and loving on your child or even allowing the child to feel seen was just not a part of her life. But she did give me Jesus. She did give me a belief in something bigger than myself. So, I am grateful for that." As a young child, the Bible was Oprah's most important book. In fact, her great-aunt named her after the biblical Orpah, a woman featured in the Old Testament's Book of Ruth. People had trouble pronouncing "Orpah," saying "Oprah" instead. The name stuck.

It was her grandfather who taught her how to actually read. Oprah described books as her "path to personal freedom." She said, "Books allowed me to see a world beyond the front porch of my grandmother's shotgun house and gave me the power to see possibilities beyond what was allowed at the time: beyond economic and social realities, beyond classrooms with no books and unqualified teachers, beyond false beliefs and prejudice that veiled the minds of so many men and women of the time. For me, those dreams started when I heard the stories of my rich heritage. When I read about Sojourner Truth and Harriet Tubman and Mary McLeod Bethune and Frederick Douglass. I knew that there was possibility for me."

At age three she started memorizing and reciting verses in church. She was invited to speak at other churches in the area. She was a natural performer and never shied away from being in the spotlight. She basked in the attention she was getting and loved making her grandmother proud. Her childhood consisted of church, chores, reading, and recitations.

When she was six, Oprah was sent to live with her mother in Milwaukee, Wisconsin. Instead of pigs and cows, Oprah made friends with cockroaches named Melinda and Sandy. Her mother, who had very little education, did not appreciate her love of reading and public speaking. According to USA Today, Oprah recalled a time when her mother snatched a book out of her hands and said, "You're nothing but a bookworm. You think you're better than the other kids." Although hurt and confused, Oprah didn't stop reading.

Oprah started kindergarten in Milwaukee and was way ahead of the other kids, who were still learning to read and write. Oprah wrote a note to her teacher: "Dear Miss New, I do not belong here because I can read, and I know a lot of big words like elephant and hippopotamus." Her teacher was convinced and moved Oprah into the first grade.

A couple of years later she temporarily went to live with her father in Nashville, Tennessee. Oprah continued to read. Her favorite books were the Strawberry Girl series by Lois Lenski. Unlike her mother, her father encouraged her reading. Oprah said, "Because of his respect for education and my stepmother's respect for education, every single week of my life that I lived with them I had to read library books and that was the beginning of the book club. Who knew? But I was reading books and had to do book reports in my own house." Oprah's stepmother read fifteen to thirty minutes a day and encouraged Oprah to do the same. Oprah said, "We would go to the library and would draw books every two weeks. I would take out five books, and I would have a little reading time every day. That's what encouraged me to become a great reader."

While still in Nashville during elementary school, she also skipped third grade. Then came a turning point: "One of the defining moments of my life came in the fourth grade, the year I was Mrs. Duncan's student. What Mrs. Duncan did for me was to help me to not be afraid of being smart. She encouraged me to read, and she often stayed after school to work with me, helping me choose books." Oprah resumed speaking in public, at church and in school, at this time. She especially loved to recite the poem "Invictus" by William Ernest Henley. Oprah didn't know what all the words meant, but she spoke them with flair, adding hand motions and really selling it.

At age seventeen—after she'd returned to her father's home for her later high school years—Oprah used her stage performance skills and won the Miss Black Tennessee beauty pageant. In doing so, she attracted the attention of a local Black radio station and was hired to do the news part-time. From then on, she worked in local media and became the youngest and first Black news anchor at a Nashville TV station. She moved to Chicago and had great success working on various talk shows. In 1986 the first episode of *The Oprah Winfrey Show* aired. The show ran for twenty-five seasons and consisted of more than 4,500 episodes. She said, "I wanted to be able to use the show to enlighten as well as entertain, to have people think differently about themselves and their lives."

Oprah never forgot about her love of reading. People trusted her, so when she told them to read, they did. In 1996 she launched Oprah's Book Club with the purpose of getting "America reading again." The club captured all types of readers and made challenging books more accessible. Oprah used her celebrity status to elevate book groups and promote reading by making it a shared experience. She discussed the books and would often invite the authors to speak on her show. She also supported libraries by making sure they had copies of her book club picks. Although in a different format, her book club still continues today.

Oprah has always enjoyed reading as part of her job. In order to select books for her book club, she reads about five books a week and loves browsing in bookstores "looking for the right book, the one you can't put down." Her goal has always been for "books to become part of my audience's lifestyle, for reading to become a natural phenomenon with them, so that it is no longer a big deal." She's also known for hosting literary salons for a select group of fans. These salons started in her home and then moved into her studio. Oprah modeled how to read and talk about books. In essence, she became American's top book influencer. She said, "Nothing, not one thing or activity, can replace the experience of a good read—being transported to a different land, a different realm, through words and language. . . . I love being surrounded by books. For me, they're like art, little pieces of sculpture placed all over the house, reminding me, always, of the power of the written word. Just looking at them brings me the purest kind of joy."

Of all people, Oprah knows the power of a good story. She knows that books themselves have great power, and she knows that there is nothing more powerful than a community of readers. She said, "Books connect us and bring us all closer."

SONIA SOLVES MYSTERIES
SONIA SOTOMAYOR (1954–)

"Through reading, I escaped the bad parts of my life in the South Bronx. And, through books, I got to travel the world and the universe. It, to me, was a passport out of my childhood and it remains a way—through the power of words—to change the world."

Sonia Sotomayor is one of the most important people in the United States, sitting on the Supreme Court, wearing cool black robes, unraveling one mystery after another. As the first Latinx person and the third woman to serve on the nation's highest court, Sonia is a champion of communities of color and a proponent of criminal justice reform.

Although Sonia is surrounded by books today, mostly about legal cases, books just weren't part of her early and difficult childhood. She grew up in a low-income New York City neighborhood, the daughter of two Puerto Rican immigrants who, at first, didn't speak much English. Her mother worked long hours outside the home, as a nurse, and her parents were constantly fighting until her father died from a heart attack hastened by his alcoholism when Sonia was nine. This left Sonia's mother with two young children to raise by herself. Sonia said, "Neglect was the right word. I barely saw my mother, and the mom I saw was often angry and unhappy."

At seven years old Sonia was diagnosed with type 1 diabetes. She had to learn how to give herself her own injections of insulin, which she needed to stay alive. She said, "I spent a good portion of my life hiding my disease. . . . [Diabetes] is really a fundamental part of me. It's part of my body; it's part of everything I do all day long—exercising, eating, stopping internally for a moment to check where my blood sugars are." Later in her childhood, Sonia found great solace in reading. She read to escape and to learn.

Once Sonia reached fifth grade, her mother became obsessed with education. She made a point of speaking English at home and was always urging, "You've got to get your education! It's the only way to get ahead in the world." At great sacrifice, she bought her children all twenty-four volumes of the *Encyclopedia Britannica*, something none of their neighbors had ever seen. After that, "The world branched out before me in a thousand new directions," Sonia recalled.

Her library card was a prized possession. Cocooning herself at the local library, she read randomly, without any particular guidance. She liked chapter books and soon discovered the Nancy Drew mysteries, starring amateur detective Nancy on the case. Sonia devoured one after another. As she solved mysteries, Nancy was cool and collected, a genius at turning obstacles to her own advantage. A daredevil action hero who lived for adventure, Nancy confronted puzzles and mysteries head-on. She was respected and brave, outspoken, kindhearted.

Sonia took Nancy Drew as a role model. She said, "I was a keen observer and listener. I picked up on clues. I figured things out logically, and I enjoyed puzzles. I loved the clear, focused feeling that came when I concentrated on solving a problem and everything else faded out. And I could be brave when I needed to be."

Sonia went to Roman Catholic schools, in such dread of the strict nuns that she seldom misbehaved. Once, for back talking, she was hauled up to the front of the cafeteria and slapped. In her classes she wasn't doing well at first, but she solved her own problem. She went to the smartest girl in her class, asked her for studying tips, and started on a path of doing well.

As a teen she volunteered to do the Bible reading in church on Sundays, something girls had only recently been allowed to do—before that it was boys only. She joined the high school debate team, sought out her brainiest friends to discuss current events, and worked constantly to get good grades.

Sonia graduated at the top of her class and won a full scholarship to Princeton University. She was one of the few Latinas on campus. She said, "Oh gosh, I was filled with fear. When you come from a background like mine, where you're entering worlds that are so different than your own, you have to be afraid." Terrified of failing, she never raised her hand in class, still hiding out at the library. She spent her summers studying grammar and vocabulary and catching up on classic books that she'd missed—she'd never heard of Lewis Carroll's *Alice in Wonderland*, for example.

In time Sonia came out of her shell. She became involved with Puerto Rican groups on campus. She established herself as a campus leader at Princeton and went on to study at Yale Law School. Sonia knew she wanted a career in law since age ten. He favorite TV show was *Perry Mason*, an American legal drama about a defense lawyer. It inspired her to be a lawyer. It also inspired her to be a judge. She said, "After the guilty party had confessed, Perry turned to the judge. And at that moment, I realized that the most important person in that room was the judge. I wanted to be that person." She was on her way to a brilliant career, solving legal mysteries as a prominent trial lawyer and rising to become a judge in the lower courts in New York.

In 2009 she made history as the first Latinx person to be appointed to the highest court in the land: the United States Supreme Court. Using the U.S. Constitution as its guide, the Supreme Court rules on cases that lower courts haven't been able to decide. These cases are, by nature, the most puzzling legal issues. But Sonia is more than ready to tackle the nation's problems. She is a woman whose early reading directly led to her accomplishments. Reading mystery books inspired her to get a job solving quandaries and seeking justice. Besides deciding on important cases, she reaches out to young people by writing books for children and giving speeches. Serving as a role model "is the most valuable thing I can do," she said. "The key to success in my life, it's the secret that I want to share with kids and how I became successful. I'm here as a Supreme Court Justice only because of books."

SERENA RISES UP

SERENA WILLIAMS (1981–)

"Every woman's success should be an inspiration to another.
We're strongest when we cheer each other on."

Serena Williams is a high-ranked American professional tennis player and the only American to have won more than twenty Grand Slam tennis tournament victories. In addition, she is a businesswoman, expanding her brand into film, television, and fashion. One of the greatest tennis players of all time, Serena Williams is a tennis goddess, along with her older sister Venus.

Their father masterminded their careers, with their mother's help. He decided when the girls were only three and four that his daughters would play championship tennis. But he also wanted them to take it slow and focus on schoolwork. If they didn't do their homework or their grades slipped, he wouldn't let them play tennis. Of her father, Serena said, "I love his strength. I love how strong he taught us to be, and not to accept anything less than what we deserve."

But tennis wasn't the Williams sisters' only passion. Serena copied her sister in all things, and when Venus turned into a big reader, Serena did too. She said, "When we weren't playing tennis, we were usually reading." Serena loves reading. She reads books to improve her vocabulary, to bolster her confidence, and to help her through life's big moments. Among her favorites are Brandon Mull's Fablehaven series and J. K. Rowling's Harry Potter books. However, the one thing she won't read is articles about herself. "Since the day I won the U.S. Open, my very first Grand Slam, I never read articles about myself. If I saw my name mentioned, I'd look away. I looked at the pictures, but that's pretty much it. I didn't want to get too cocky, and at the same time, I didn't want to have that negative energy."

Serena's interests have gone far beyond tennis. In college she studied fashion, business, and pre-med. She speaks French fluently and spends much of her time in Paris. She said, "One of the reasons I learned French was I wanted to win the French Open, and I wanted to speak French when I won. The second was because, most African countries, the main language outside of their local language is French or English. So I figured: I know English, maybe I can learn French." (One of her life goals is to go to Africa, "to see my roots, where I'm from.")

Throughout her wins and losses, her favorite author and major inspiration has been the African American poet and autobiographer Maya Angelou. She loved reading *I Know Why the Caged Bird Sings*, the true story of Maya growing up in the segregated rural South. In lines from Maya's poems and speeches, Serena has always found encouragement: "I'm a woman, phenomenally. Phenomenal woman, that's me"; "Each time a woman stands up for herself . . . she stands up for all women"; "A wise woman wishes to be no one's enemy; a wise woman refuses to be anyone's victim"; and "I love to see a young girl go out and grab the world by the lapels."

From an early age, the Williams sisters were trained by their father to write down their hopes and goals. Serena got in the habit of doing this on a regular basis. She keeps a journal and writes Angelou-like notes to herself before every tennis match. The notes are variations on the same five messages: "Stay positive"; "Believe you can do anything, even when down"; "Focus on every point"; "You are the best, Serena"; and "Believe it, act it, become it."

The sisters soared to record-breaking heights. Sometimes they even battled each other, which was a stressful time for them and their mother, who said, "I can't root for either one because I don't want either one to get mad at me . . . especially Serena. Venus will be able to handle it, but Serena, no."

In the midst of her success Serena also faced many obstacles and hardships. She said, "I lived through tragedies and controversies. People look down on me, put me down because I didn't look like them. I look stronger. I've had people look past me because of the color of my skin. I've had people overlook me because I [am] a woman." She was dogged by vicious sexist and racist insults. Her guard had to be up at all times, especially as she became too famous to live a normal life. She became a commenter on social issues, striving to be a positive influence on young girls and boys who see her as a role model and an ambassador of tennis. She said, "I can't look at my daughter and tell her I sat back and was quiet. No! She will know how to stand up for herself and others—through my example."

She spoke out after a discovery when shopping for baby clothes. The girls' clothes were labeled with things like MOMMY'S PRINCESS and DADDY'S PRINCESS. The boys' clothes, on the other hand, were labeled with sayings like CURIOUS, I AM A THINKER, I AM SMART, or I CAN DO ANYTHING. Serena was appalled at the different messages for girls versus boys, saying the time is now "to start instilling that positive [message], telling your daughter, 'You can do anything. You can be the best.' It's just the way we tell our sons." Serena wants her daughter to know she can rise as high as she wants to.

Always, Serena comes back to Maya Angelou for strength and inspiration. She recites her all-time favorite poem, "Still I Rise," in public whenever she has the chance: "You may shoot me with your words, / You may cut me with your eyes, / You may kill me with your hatefulness, / But still, like air, I'll rise."

As energetic as she is on the court, Serena is just as active in giving her money away. Her nonprofit organization has funded schools in Jamaica, Kenya, and Uganda, where she sometimes helps with the actual construction. Because only boys are sometimes sent to school in Africa, Serena made a commitment to educate boys and girls equally: "We had a strict rule that our schools had to be at least 40 percent girls."

The stunning success of the Williams sisters has been credited with launching a new era of power tennis for women. In Serena's words, "We must continue to dream big, and in doing so, we empower the next generation of women to be just as bold in their pursuits."

TAYLOR SHAKES IT OFF

TAYLOR SWIFT (1989–)

"I wanna say to all the young women out there, there are going to be people along the way who will try to undercut your success or take credit for your accomplishments or your fame. But if you just focus on the work, and you don't let those people sidetrack you, someday when you get where you're going, you'll look around and you will know that it was you and the people who loved you who put you there. And that will be the greatest feeling in the world."

Taylor Swift songs can be heard almost anywhere. Taylor is one of the greatest and most prolific songwriters of twenty-first-century pop and country music. She grew up in Wyomissing, Pennsylvania; before that, she lived on her family's Christmas tree farm (the origins of her 2019 song "Christmas Tree Farm").

She was named after the musician James Taylor. From the start, Taylor loved words, singing, and performing. She said, "I think I fell in love with words before I fell in love with music. All I wanted to do was talk and all I wanted to do was hear stories." At age three she would walk up to strangers and sing songs from *The Lion King*. She would watch movies and just remember the songs. She sang hymns in church. At age six Taylor was given her first album: *Blue* by LeAnn Rimes. From that moment, Taylor was hooked on country music. She listened to Dolly Parton, Patsy Cline, Shania Twain, Faith Hill, and the Chicks.

In school Taylor excelled at poetry and writing. When given an assignment to write a two-sentence essay, Taylor submitted two pages. One of her teachers said, "Even as early as first grade, she was using positional phrases unheard of from kids that age." At age ten Taylor won a poetry contest for her "Monster in My Closet." She said, "Poetry was my favorite thing. I loved putting things down on paper. It was so fascinating to me." Poetry and songwriting were safe spaces for Taylor—she was bullied and teased at school for supposedly being awkward, annoying, and too tall. "I first started writing songs because I didn't really have anyone else to talk to," she said. "Songwriting for me just started out as therapy."

Feeling different from her peers who were more interested in parties and dating, Taylor became a bit of a loner, preferring to make art. But being a loner actually benefited her, as she became a keen observer of the life around her. She used these observations and her inner struggles to write her songs. She learned to play the guitar at age twelve. Armed with poetry and music, she used her art as a way to heal, as a way to shake off the negativity. Some of her song lyrics were "lines you wish you could text-message somebody in real life." She said, "I would just be constantly writing all these zingers—like, 'Burn. That would really get her.'" At age fourteen Taylor wrote a 350-page unpublished novel called *Girl Named Girl* about a mother who wants a son but instead has a daughter.

Taylor is also a huge reader. She particularly enjoys books with happy endings and moral messages. She said, "Being good to other people was the main concept I really loved in books." Growing up, she liked funny books like Peggy Parish's Amelia Bedelia series or sentimental books like Shel Silverstein's *The Giving Tree*. In the fifth grade she read Lois Lowry's *The Giver*, and years later she starred as one of the characters in the movie version of the book. One of her favorite authors is John Green, who writes bestselling young adult novels like *The Fault in Our Stars*, *Paper Towns*, and *Looking for Alaska*.

Taylor is very inspired by reading great literary works: "You hear storytelling like in Harper Lee's *To Kill a Mockingbird* and it just . . . it makes your mind wander. It makes you feel like it makes your world more vast. And you think about more things and greater concepts after you read something like that." Her reading often shows up in her songs. For example, "Love Story" references William Shakespeare's *Romeo and Juliet* and Nathaniel Hawthorne's *The Scarlet Letter*. In her songs she has also alluded to Charlotte Brontë's *Jane Eyre*, F. Scott Fitzgerald's *The Great Gatsby*, Daphne du Maurier's *Rebecca*, Lewis Carroll's *Alice in Wonderland*, J. M. Barrie's *Peter Pan*, Charles Dickens's *A Tale of Two Cities*, Kurt Vonnegut's *Slaughterhouse-Five*, and more. She has also referenced poets such as Emily Dickinson, William Wordsworth, and Robert Frost. Paying homage to E. E. Cummings's lowercase poetry, her *folklore* and *evermore* albums are in lower case.

Starting at about age nine, Taylor got involved with musical theater and took singing and acting lessons. All of it led her to the life of a musician. She said, "I was infatuated with the sound, with the storytelling. I could relate to it. . . . I wanted to sing country music." She started singing at karaoke bars and at county fairs. At around age fourteen she made her own demo, moved to Nashville, Tennessee, with her family, and landed a recording contract. Her first single was "Tim McGraw," which was about one of Taylor's favorite country music stars. The song became a hit and catapulted Taylor onto the main stage. She found herself touring and putting out one hit album after another. The once-upon-a-time loner is now a worldwide superstar with legions of fans known as "Swifties."

Taylor is a prolific and talented songwriter; yet, like other successful women, her skills have been questioned. She has been accused of not writing her own songs. She said, "it's a feminist issue. My friend [Ed Sheeran], no one questions whether he writes everything. . . . It's a little discouraging that females have to work so much harder to prove that they do their own things. I see Nicki Minaj and Iggy Azalea having to prove that they write their own raps or their own lyrics, and it makes me sad, because they shouldn't have to justify it."

Taylor is a world-famous celebrity. Her concerts have been known to sell out in less than two minutes. She is an award-winning, chart-topping, and record-breaking performing artist. As a singer, songwriter, actress, and one of the youngest highest-paid celebrities in history, she's had great success. Since she herself benefited from music education, she funded the Taylor Swift Education Center at the Country Music Hall of Fame in Nashville. As a booklover, she has supported libraries in Wyomissing and Nashville.

Her key to success? According to Taylor, "I surround myself with smart, beautiful, passionate, driven, ambitious women. Other women who are killing it should motivate you, thrill you, challenge you and inspire you rather than threaten you and make you feel like you're immediately being compared to them. The only thing I compare myself to is me, two years ago, or me one year ago. . . . You just try to lead by example, and you hope, someday, that if we talk about feminism enough, maybe we'll start to actually see it make a difference in the way young girls perceive themselves and each other."

MALALA DOESN'T BACK DOWN
MALALA YOUSAFZAI (1997–)

"Books can capture injustices in a way that stays with you
and makes you want to do something about them. That's why they are so powerful."

Malala Yousafzai is a Pakistani activist who fights for the right of every child to get an education. She has become the international symbol for girls' education. Malala was born in northern Pakistan in Swat Valley and proudly calls herself "bookish." Her father, a staunch advocate for female education who founded and taught at a girls' school, was determined to give Malala all the opportunities that a boy would have. As a young girl, Malala loved listening to her father tell stories about their Pashtun culture. She also loved it when he recited poems, sometimes crying as he read. From an early age, Malala fell in love with learning and books. Before she could even talk, she found herself in her father's school pretending to be the teacher. (Imagine her standing in front of the room, pointing at her imaginary class and using books as props.) It's no surprise that she was an advanced learner. When she started school at age three or four, she was placed in classes for much older children.

When the Taliban, a terrorist group, took control of Malala's village, they banned many things, including owning a television, playing music, sending girls to schools, and reading books (especially those from Europe and the Americas). Homes were raided. Books and computers were confiscated. Schools were bombed. Acid was thrown in girls' faces if they attempted to go to school. Malala said, "The terrorists showed what frightens them most: a girl with a book."

Like other girls her age at that time, Malala was obsessed with the Twilight books by Stephenie Meyer. When the Taliban came to her village when she was ten, she said they "arrived in the night just like vampires." She added, "Sometimes I think it's easier to be a Twilight vampire than a girl in Swat." Malala related to Meyer's characters' need to hide in plain sight: as a girl who wanted to read and learn in a Taliban-controlled region, she was an outsider in her own home.

Malala and others found a way to defy the Taliban by hiding books. She would hide her books under her bed and read in secret. She read any book she could get her hands on. Favorites included *The Alchemist* by Paulo Coelho, *Anna Karenina* by Leo Tolstoy, Jane Austen novels, and books about Martin Luther King, Jr. Although her reading choices were (and still are) pretty eclectic, she preferred nonfiction, especially autobiographies. She also liked to read novels that reflect the real world.

Books kept her sane and gave her peace. In reading Stephen Hawking's *A Brief History of Time*, she said, "I distracted myself from the fear and terrorism by thinking about things like how the universe began and whether time travel is possible. I enjoy science, and I'm a very curious person. I always want to know the reason behind everything, big and small." When she decorated her hands with henna for weddings and holidays, she drew math and chemistry formulas instead of flowers and butterflies.

Malala refused to give up her books. She didn't want to give in. "I want to get my education and I want to become a doctor," she stated. "They cannot fully stop me. I will continue to learn if it's at home, school, or somewhere else." When the Taliban allowed girls in the early elementary grades to attend school again, Malala pretended to be younger so that she could continue going to school. To avoid being harassed on her way there, she wore ordinary plain clothes instead of her uniform and concealed her books in her shawl.

A BBC news correspondent in Pakistan who knew Malala's father approached her about writing a blog to document the oppression that was happening in Pakistan. Malala wrote under the pen name Gul Makai, a Pashtun folk hero, and shared what it was like being a girl under Taliban rule. Her first blog was titled "I Am Afraid." What she was doing was dangerous, as the Taliban would surely punish anyone who publicly spoke against them. For a while Malala was able to keep her identity a secret. But she started speaking up in public. She spoke at local events. Her speeches were publicized in local newspapers and on TV. Malala and her father felt like they "needed to stand up."

Her activism made her a target. In 2012, when she was on her way home from school, a masked gunman boarded her bus and shot her on the left side of her face. She was so badly injured that she had to be flown to a hospital in England. She endured months of surgeries and rehabilitation. Once again, reading gave her some peace. She said, "*The Wonderful Wizard of Oz* was the first book I read in the hospital. . . . It is a lovely book, and it was given to me by [former British prime minister] Gordon Brown—he sent me 25 books, and this was my favorite."

Malala didn't back down. She recovered and read on. She would not allow the Taliban to defeat her. She continued to fight for girls' education. She also continued her own education. Since it was too dangerous for Malala to return to Pakistan, she went to school in England at Oxford University. While there, she kept reading. "In university my favorite was Plato's *The Republic*. I could talk about it for hours." She said, "If I had the option, I could sit for months and read. Just read, read, and read."

In 2020 she started her own book club, named "Fearless." She said, "I believe reading together is a great way to connect with and learn about people." In addition, she hosts more intimate book clubs with her friends, especially friends from Pakistan and India. She said, "We're focusing on books in South Asia, and it's quite extraordinary to focus on books from your region."

Malala has become a much-admired education activist. "Together," she believes, "we can create a world where all girls can learn and lead." She travels across the world meeting and fighting for girls' education. She speaks out against the many barriers girls face, including poverty, war, child marriage, and gender discrimination. In 2013 she started the Malala Fund to support girls' education. In 2014 Malala received the Nobel Peace Prize for her work, becoming the youngest person ever to receive the prize. She donated her prize money to start a new school for girls in Pakistan.

Malala is often called a "warrior of words." The United Nations designated her birthday, July 12, as Malala Day. She said, "Malala Day is not my day. Today is the day of every woman, every boy, and every girl who have raised their voice for their rights." A formidable force, Malala reminds us of the power of education: "Let us wage a global struggle against illiteracy, poverty, and terrorism. Let us pick up our books and our pens. They are our most powerful weapons."

AMANDA CLIMBS HILLS

AMANDA GORMAN (1998–)

"Books have the power to change how we see ourselves and others.
The choice is ours to harness that potential."

Amanda Gorman has a powerful voice—a voice of the past, present, and future. With spirit and style, she is making poetry cool. She rose to fame when she read her poem "The Hill We Climb" at President Joe Biden's inauguration in 2021. Twenty-two at the time, she was the youngest poet to perform at a U.S. presidential inauguration. She's also the first National Youth Poet Laureate and the first person to be commissioned to write a poem to read at the Super Bowl.

Before all the lyrical glitz and glam, Amanda had to climb her own hills. As a young girl living in Los Angeles, California, she struggled with learning disabilities. Born prematurely, she suffered from many ear infections as a baby. She developed an auditory processing disorder, which means that even though she could hear sounds, her brain took longer to make sense of them. She also had a speech impediment and could not form certain sounds, like *r*. Up until her twenties, she even struggled with saying her own last name correctly. This made Amanda self-conscious about speaking. She preferred to read and write instead. Luckily, her mother was a teacher, so Amanda received a lot of support, including speech therapy.

For Amanda, her communication struggles helped her become a better poet. She said, "For a long time, I looked at it as a weakness. Now I really look at it as a strength because going through that process, it made me a writer, for one, because I had to find a form in which I could communicate other than through my mouth, and two, when I was brave enough to try to take those words from the page onto the stage, I brought with me this understanding of the complexity of sound, pronunciation, emphasis."

Although she read and spoke later than other kids due to her learning difficulties, she practiced and practiced until she mastered reading, writing, and speaking. She said, "I had to put in the work, the labor." One of her practice activities was to repeatedly listen and sing the song "Aaron Burr, Sir" from the musical *Hamilton* by Lin-Manuel Miranda. She learns a lot from music, which is a form of poetry. She sees instrumental composers as "great storytellers" able to tell stories with music, not words. Amanda loves figuring out the meanings of wordless songs for herself. (Amanda admits that no one in her family, including herself, can actually sing.)

She first fell in love with words in the third grade, when her teacher introduced her to poetry and metaphor. She realized her writing "could flower into something much bigger." Because of her communication issues, she was entranced by poetry's ability to say a lot with a little. She wrote her first poems about feeling like an outsider among kids her own age. Teachers encouraged her to develop her poetry. In middle school she was introduced to Sonia Sanchez's book of poetry *Shake Loose My Skin*, remembering, "I fell in love with it and reread it every day." She also read *Angles of Ascent: A Norton Anthology of Contemporary African American Poetry*. Of that book, she said, "I just had this feeling of, 'Oh, these are my people.'"

Amanda was also inspired by Toni Morrison's *The Bluest Eye* and Ray Bradbury's *Dandelion Wine*. She said these books "jump-started" her interest in writing as a craft: "When I came across these works as a young reader, I so deeply wanted to understand how these writers had arrived at these stories." She was also especially moved by Maya Angelou, who also struggled with speech. "I felt like Maya was me growing up. She overcame years of not speaking up for herself, all for the love of poetry." Other poets she admires include Gwendolyn Brooks, Lucille Clifton, Federico García Lorca, Rainer Maria Rilke, and Octavia E. Butler. She also counts these writers among her favorites: Ocean Vuong, Clint Smith, Madeline Miller, Jeremy O. Harris, and Roxane Gay. She likes to read fantasy, thrillers, and young adult novels like Angie Thomas's *The Hate U Give*. She has said she's too much of a "wimp" to read horror stories.

Throughout her youth, Amanda kept reading and allowed her reading to inform her writing. At age five she would wake up early to write fan fiction. She said her mother had to pay her a quarter to sleep in past five a.m. Her first long-form writings were centered on "white girls with red hair and blue eyes, very *Anne of Green Gables*" (by L. M. Montgomery). It wasn't until she read Toni Morrison in middle school that she realized "that stories could actually be about people who look like me." Then, in high school, she read Audre Lorde and Phillis Wheatley and realized poetry could be a tool to address social justice issues. She kept practicing her craft, writing more and more stories and poems. While still in high school Amanda submitted a poem and was selected as the Los Angeles Youth Poet Laureate in 2014. She published her first book of poems titled *The One for Whom Food Is Not Enough* in 2015. This set her on a path to poetic stardom.

As a young Black woman, Amanda wants poetry to be more inclusive. She said, "We really need to break out of the pathology that poetry is only owned by certain elites. Where we can start is highlighting and celebrating poets who reflect humanity in all of its diverse colors and breadth." Amanda sings the praises of poets of color. "I love Black poets. I love that as a Black girl, I get to participate in that legacy. So that's Yusef Komunyakaa, Sonia Sanchez, Tracy K. Smith, Phillis Wheatley."

When not writing, Amanda can be found reading. She describes her happy place as one with a fireplace crackling nearby, warm tea in her hands, a blanket over her lap, and "a thick, well-loved book" in her hands. She also loves rereading books: "If I read something once, I tend to reread it at least three times. There's some I return to for the craft they can teach me." Two books that she says are always on her nightstand and that she could read every night are Ron Chernow's *Alexander Hamilton* and Shakespeare's *Othello*. Regarding Shakespeare, Amanda had to learn to like him, saying that he "just felt like another ancient dead white guy that my teachers were trying to shove into my brain when I was desperate to read someone who looked like me. When I was in college, I had this moment of thinking: If you're going to close yourself off to an author, at least read them to understand why. I owed that to myself and to literature." So she took a course about Shakespeare and was hooked. "I think it was finally being able to read Shakespeare through a global, racial and gendered lens that made me see him anew."

For Amanda, poetry is a way for her to express herself: "When I think about what I'm most afraid to write about it's about me and my life. . . . There's a lot of things that make up the shape of who we are and rather than trying to change those parts, I'm just trying to invite them in and write them down." Writing is also a vehicle for her activism. She said, "Poetry and language are often at the heartbeat of movements for change. . . . Never underestimate the power of art as the language of the people." Amanda is a voice for racial justice and cultural reckoning. When she spoke at President Biden's inauguration, the whole world heard her voice. When writing the inaugural poem, she learned from reading a lot of Frederick Douglass, Winston Churchill, and Abraham Lincoln—all great orators.

Inspired by all the authors and books she has read, she is poised to inspire future poets and writers who are committed to climbing hills and advocating for racial justice. She closed her inaugural poem with these words: "For there is always light, if only we're brave enough to see it. If only we're brave enough to be it."

MARLEY GETS IT DONE

MARLEY DIAS (2005–)

"We live in an unfair world and we have to fight."

Marley Dias saw a problem and did something about it. At age ten she became an education activist while eating pancakes with her mother after school. In between bites, she complained about being assigned to read *Where the Red Fern Grows* by Wilson Rawls. She later explained, "It is one of those 'classic books' that's existed in our school systems for so long. My great-grandparents remember when that book came out. I read it last year and it was still assigned. Every single year they wanted us to read a book about a white boy and his dog." Marley was also required to read *Shiloh* by Phyllis Reynolds Naylor and *Old Yeller* by Fred Gipson—more books about white boys and their dogs.

Marley learned to read at age two. She proudly calls herself a TBN, or "total book nerd." In her self-selected recreational reading, she read about diverse characters. But school was a different story. Her school-assigned reading was all about white people. She couldn't connect with the characters. She wanted to see herself reflected in books. She was super frustrated. She used this frustration for good, saying, "Frustration is fuel that can lead to the development of an innovative and useful idea."

She led a social media campaign to promote diverse books. In 2015 she launched #1000BlackGirlBooks to give kids "a stronger sense of identity." Her goal was to collect and donate one thousand books featuring Black female protagonists. (She ended up collecting over ten thousand.) She wanted to send the books to the school her mother attended in Jamaica as a child. She said, "Even in all-Black spaces like Jamaica, where it is majority Black people, they don't see themselves, and the narratives of white people are still being

pushed onto people." She is driven by her love for books: "I am doing this because I love to read, I love books, I love being here, I am passionate."

The first two books she collected were Kelly DiPucchio's *Grace for President* and Jacqueline Woodson's *Brown Girl Dreaming*, the latter of which she cites as one of her favorite books. Her aunt had given her Woodson's book as a birthday present. The book introduced Marley to a whole new world. She described this new world as one in which "modern Black girls were the main characters—not invisible, not just the sidekick. A world where Black girls were free to be complicated, honest, human; to have adventures and emotions unique just to them. A world where Black girls' stories mattered." Marley's project was all about representing and including the experiences and voices of Black females. She said she wanted to "see my own story reflected in the books I have to read."

One of the major perks of #1000BlackGirlBooks was that Marley got to read all kinds of books. She discovered a love for Nigerian American author Tomi Adeyemi, who writes fantasy stories about Black people "in futuristic and magical space." Marley appreciates how Black authors like Tomi disrupt white spaces and include people of color. She said, "For the Black kids out there, who really love fantasy but never see themselves, they now feel a whole new level of connection. That's important."

Marley's mission was more than just a book drive. She wanted to improve lives by providing much-needed diverse books to underserved communities. She donated books to schools and libraries. She developed a resource guide to help people find books. She talked to teachers and lawmakers about the need to increase diverse books. She hosted book fairs. She finds the lack of literary representation problematic, noting, "This gap hurts all of us. I'm working to create a space where it feels easy to include and imagine Black girls and make Black girls like me the main characters of our lives."

Marley is constantly learning from books. For example, from Audre Lorde, she learned about speechwriting. She said, "I've become more interested in talking about social injustice and my own perspective in a bit more of a confident way that Audre Lorde is known for. I'm really interested in learning more about how Black women who have come before me have been able to really command an audience and speak truth to power through their speeches."

Marley is often asked about book recommendations. "For younger kids, I would recommend *The Story of Ruby Bridges* [by Robert Coles] and *No Mirrors in My Nana's House* [by Ysaye M. Barnwell]. For kids in 2nd or 3rd grade, I would recommend the Dear America series. Most of the stories in the Dear America series, if they have Black girls, are about them being enslaved, but they escape or do something really adventurous. But for people in 4th through 6th grade, I would recommend *Chains* by Laurie Halse Anderson, *Brown Girl Dreaming* by Jacqueline Woodson, and *Roll of Thunder, Hear My Cry* [by Mildred D. Taylor]."

Marley was recognized by *Time* magazine as one of the most influential teens. She has given many speeches and appeared on many talk shows. She's also the host and executive producer of Netflix's *Bookmarks: Celebrating Black Voices*. For Marley, books have come full circle—she has transitioned from reader to author. At age eleven she wrote an autobiography and activist guidebook called *Marley Dias Gets It Done: And So Can You!* She describes it as a "wish for a better tomorrow." She wrote, "I hope that when you read this book—or any book at all—it will feel like you are giving yourself a gift that you're excited to share. . . . There's more to a book than just reading it." She opened her book with this statement: "If only there'd been one book at school . . . just one . . . about a Black girl and her dog."

KATHY READS ON THE JOB

KATHLEEN KRULL (1952–2021)

"There is no such thing as reading too much."

In January 2021, Kathleen Krull (or Kathy, to those who knew her) passed away. This book is dedicated to her, with all my heart. Kathy was a dear friend and mentor to me. We shared a love for reading, piano, and gossip! (Kathy always wanted to know "what the neighbors thought.") We were in a book club and a piano recital club together for many years. Kathy was one of my most favorite people in the whole world. I feel grateful for every moment I was able to be a part of her big, shiny light. She dedicated two of her books to me. A woman of many talents and superpowers, she respected, promoted, and amplified other women whenever she could.

Kathy was a pioneer in the children's book world. She started as a book editor and an in-house author. Then she transitioned into being a full-time children's book author who "mastered the art of writing high-interest informational books for children." Having written more than one hundred books, she made children's nonfiction "cool," which was one of her favorite words—"dude" was another favorite.

She used to say, "Nonfiction picture book biographies have been good to me." But the truth is that Kathy was good for children's nonfiction. She helped popularize this genre and got it out of required school reading assignments and into nighttime story selections. She humanized historical figures with "solid research, lively writing, and juicy 'gossip.'" She said, "Gossip is a way for kids to learn about history, by using gossipy details about people from the past. It's a way to hook readers in." She loved gossip so much that when she was about twelve, she wrote a research paper about the word "gossip." An award-winning author, she dazzled readers of all ages with fun facts and titillating tittle-tattle about famous people.

By the second grade Kathy was writing short stories and poems. Her first book was about a garden. In fifth grade she wrote a book called *Hair-Do's and People I Know*. (She kept this manuscript and had it laminated. She would share it at her author visits.) In sixth grade she created a series of "weird little books about people." In middle school, for a school assignment, she wrote a short story about a nun who jumps out a window, falling to her death. She titled it "Death Waits Until After Dark." (It is important to note here that Kathy went to Catholic schools taught by nuns, whom she liked and respected. So she herself didn't understand why her story went so "dark.") Her teacher, who of course was a nun, asked her to reconsider the ending but gave her an A for writing well. Kathy credits her teachers for encouraging her writing skills. She was a big fan of teachers and librarians and nuns.

The first book Kathy remembered reading was Robert Louis Stevenson's *A Child's Garden of Verses*. Growing up, she also read the Little Golden Books and "inexpensive editions of classics." Among her favorite childhood books were Laura Ingalls Wilder's Little House series, Elizabeth Speare's *Calico Captive* and *The Witch of Blackbird Pond*, the Landmark Book series about famous people (she especially loved reading anything about queens), Enid Blyton's Famous Five series, romances by Mary Stolz and Betty Cavanna, Scott O'Dell's *Island of the Blue Dolphins*, Louise Fitzhugh's *Harriet the Spy*, Astrid Lindgren's *Pippi Longstocking*, and fantasy books by Edward Eager and Carol Kendall.

Kathy and I shared very similar reading interests. The one book we disagreed on was L. M. Montgomery's *Anne of Green Gables*—I love this book and Kathy did not. I remember she asked me, "Why in the world do you like this book so much?" True friends can disagree about books and still love each other.

In regard to writing craft, she was inspired by Jean Fritz, whom she considered to be "the master of this field, who uses such a light touch to keep readers turning pages." Kathy was always reading and watching shows and movies to get ideas and to improve her own writing. (We had many discussions about clever plot twists and funny dialogue.)

The library was probably her favorite place in the world. She fondly remembered her weekly visits to the library with her mother, describing them as a "highlight of [my] childhood." As an adult, her love of libraries continued. She spent hours in the library, reading and researching. She would make photocopies of significant passages and book covers—this was so she could track down her research. She claimed to "read like a detective" for the "good parts." She mostly read secondary sources, scouring them for "juicy details that make information come alive." She described research for a book as a "mountain": "I research tons of material, gleaning a mountain of stuff I think is most interesting, and then revise, tinker, revise, edit, whittle, and then do some more revising to get what I hope is the very tiptop of the mountain."

Kathy's last completed published book was *Walking Toward Peace: The True Story of a Brave Woman Called Peace Pilgrim* (Flyaway Books, 2021). But that was not her last book. When she passed, she left behind many ideas and several unfinished manuscripts. This book is one of those unfinished manuscripts. She developed the concept and wrote three of the profiles: Cleopatra, Sonia Sotomayor, and Serena Williams. One of her original titles for this book was *A Girl with A Book: A Celebration of Girls Reading*. She was inspired by Malala Yousafzai's quote: "The terrorists showed what frightens them most: a girl with a book."

I was honored to be asked to complete this book for Kathy. (Many thanks to her longtime agent and friend Susan Cohen, with Writers House, for recommending me. And many thanks to respected publisher Paula Wiseman, for supporting me.) Working on this book was a way for me to be with my dear friend again. She left behind a pile of notes, printed emails, and research articles with notes in the margins. In one of her notes she wrote that she had been "collecting this material during the last 20 years." Seeing her handwritten annotations made me feel close to her, as if she was still pointing me in the right direction.

Kathy wanted to write this book for "anyone who treasures and buys books" and anyone who wants to "champion girls." According to her notes, she seemed to be inspired by two main things. First, Kathy collected art images of girls with books. She said, "Images of women reading are some of the most compelling in art history—people seem to love looking at a woman with a book (an irony when many women have had to fight for the right to read or keep their reading a secret).” Second, Kathy was a powerful feminist and a huge lover of books, so a book about women who loved to read just made sense. Kathy's house is filled with books. As mentioned earlier, she was also a regular patron of local libraries, checking out heaps of books at a time. She was always reading and always recommending books to read. (I will miss the random emails she used to send with links to books she thought I should read and also piano-themed clothes she thought I should buy.) She kept a journal in which she jotted down books to read. She also used to give away books all the time. She said, “I'm always sharing books with the neighbors—whether they want me to or not—so they think of me as a book person.”

One of my favorite stories about Kathy is about how she got fired from working at a library. As a teen, she got a job shelving books. But evidently, Kathy was awful at it. She spent more time reading books than shelving them. Needless to say, Kathy was asked to pursue another line of work. Lucky for us, she eventually became a children's book writer—for which reading books is a requirement of the job.

An eclectic reader, no book was safe from Kathy. There is no doubt in my mind that Kathleen Krull, author extraordinaire, was born reading. And now she is resting and reading in peace, hopefully surrounded by piles and piles of books, in the library of her dreams.

FEMINIST FUN FACTS

CLEOPATRA (69–30 BC)

A feminist icon, Cleopatra fought for her own power. She refused to take her husband's name. She had her own portraits made. She even had her image imprinted on the front of coins, signaling that she was the dominant ruler.

WU ZETIAN (624–705)

During her fifty-year rule Wu Zetian worked to elevate the status of women. For example, she extended the mourning period for a mother to equal that of a father. She led one of the first women's marches. She took a group of women to Mount Tai and conducted rituals that were traditionally performed by men.

QUEEN ELIZABETH I (1533–1603)

Queen Elizabeth I is the only English queen never to marry. She had many offers and was expected to marry to secure the succession. But she famously refused to do so, not wanting to give her power away to a man. She also wanted to protect England's security, so it would remain independent and free from foreign influence. She claimed to be married to England. She said, "Better beggar woman and single, than queen and married."

SOR (SISTER) JUANA INÉS DE LA CRUZ (1651–1695)

Sor Juana Inés de la Cruz was a protofeminist. She was writing about feminist ideas before feminism was a known concept. For instance, her famous text "Response to Sister Filotea" is often thought to be the first feminist manifesto. In it she fought for a woman's right to education. One of her famous poems is called "Foolish Men," which claimed that men who criticize women are illogical.

PHILLIS WHEATLEY PETERS (1753–1784)

Phillis Wheatley Peters was the first African American, the first enslaved person, and one of the first American women to be a published poet. She was one of the few women who publicly engaged in the political conversations of the time.

E. PAULINE JOHNSON (1861–1913)

E. Pauline Johnson was among the first Canadian poets to write passionately about camping and canoeing. A skilled camper and paddler, she broke down stereotypes about women in the wilderness. During her touring days, between 1890 and 1897, she paddled on many rivers, crossed many lakes, and camped in many places. She published many articles in outdoor recreation magazines, promoting an image of young, healthy women pursuing outdoor interests.

CHIEN-SHIUNG WU (1912–1997)

Chien-Shiung Wu broke through white male traditions in science. She was the first woman and first person of color to serve as president of the American Physical Society. She was also the first woman to receive an honorary doctorate from Princeton University. During her lifetime none of the top research universities in the U.S. had a female physics professor. Even today, fewer women earn degrees in physics than in other science fields.

INDIRA GANDHI (1917–1984)

In a letter to an American friend, Indira Gandhi wrote, "I believe in women being able to do everything." In 1946 she helped set up the Congress Party's Women's Section. She encouraged women to involve themselves in politics.

SHIRLEY CHISHOLM (1924–2005)

While at Brooklyn College, Shirley Chisholm was not welcome in the social clubs. Instead of trying to get into these all-white groups, she formed her own group, a sorority-like Black women students' society called Ipothia, which stood for "in pursuit of the highest in all."

PATSY MINK (1927–2002)

Patsy Mink fought tirelessly to improve the lives of women. In addition to spearheading Title IX, she also passed the Early Childhood Education Act and the Women's Educational Equity Act. She knew firsthand how hard it is for women to have careers and raise children, so she supported laws that provided childcare.

AUDRE LORDE (1934–1992)

Growing up, Audre Lorde and her sisters would sit around their kitchen table doing homework. As an adult, Audre and other writers founded a feminist publishing company named Kitchen Table: Women of Color Press. This press was devoted to promoting the works of feminist and lesbian of color writers who were denied access to other publishers. It was founded by and for women with the goal of publishing voices that were often silenced. The press ended shortly after Audre's death.

TEMPLE GRANDIN (1947–)

In 2017 Temple Grandin was inducted in the National Women's Hall of Fame. Temple has succeeded in a largely male-dominated field. She is a strong champion for women in the sciences. She said, "One of the things that motivated me was that I wanted to prove I could do it. . . . I had to make myself twice as good as the guys." She advises being an "expert" on a specific topic so that people are forced to respect your knowledge.

SALLY RIDE (1951–2012)

When she was young, Sally Ride wanted to play shortstop for the Los Angeles Dodgers. She learned she couldn't because she was a girl, so she turned to tennis instead. She became a highly ranked junior player in the U.S. and was encouraged to pursue a professional tennis career. But Sally chose science, realizing "that my education, science, was more important to me than tennis was." She committed herself to encouraging girls to study and pursue science and math.

OPRAH WINFREY (1954–)

As a survivor of child abuse herself, Oprah Winfrey fights to protect women and children. She helped champion the National Child Protection Act signed into law by President Bill Clinton in 1993. It created a national registry of child abusers that helps employers and childcare services screen out dangerous people.

MORE GIRLS WITH BOOKS

It was hard to select just twenty women to feature in this book. For the final list the editors and I aimed to be comprehensive and inclusive. That stated, there were so many other awesome women we wanted to include. Kathy had suggested several of them spotlighted below.

PRINCESS ENHEDUANNA (2285–2250 BCE): Living in ancient Iraq, Enheduanna was a princess and the high priestess of Nanna the moon god. She is the earliest known writer and poet in history. She wrote hymns and poems on clay tablets, creating content for people to read. Many people across northern and southern Mesopotamia read her writings; this helped unite the kingdoms into the world's first great empire.

MURASAKI SHIKIBU (C. 973–1014): After going on a pilgrimage to a Japanese temple, Murasaki was inspired to write *The Tale of Genji*, the world's first novel. By cleverly listening through a closed door to her brother's Chinese lessons, Murasaki secretly learned to read in Chinese, which was forbidden to Japanese women. In turn, she gave the Japanese empress lessons in reading Chinese poetry. Later the dull life at court almost squashed her, except when she read aloud to the other women. This is where she came to life. Her stories, which were about emotions and not battles, made her and others feel less alone and less trapped.

HILDEGARDE OF BINGEN (1098–1179): From age eight, Hildegard lived in a convent, hidden away from the world with other nuns. She found the convent to be a place of peace during a time of war. For her, it was just the spot for all her reading. She started with the Bible. Even though she didn't always agree with what it said about women, she kept studying it. She became the most learned woman of the Middle Ages. She was also a composer of gorgeous music and a healer familiar with all the medical books of her day.

QUEEN ELEANOR OF AQUITAINE (1122–1204): Eleanor was the Duchess of Aquitaine in her own right and became queen consort of France and later queen of England. Luckily, a tip-top education got her ready for the job. Her very favorite books were collections of romantic poetry. She also liked to read books that showed respect for women. As the most powerful woman in Europe during the Middle Ages, she changed ideas about women, promoting the chivalrous tradition in which men treated women well. She also supported many poets and writers.

SOFONISBA ANGUISSOLA (1532–1625): An Italian Renaissance painter born in northern Italy, Sofonisba was the first female artist to achieve international fame. She paved the way for other females to study art as a profession. She changed the way artists painted people. People traveled to Italy just to see Sofonisba and her five bookish, artsy sisters. When they weren't drawing and painting, the girls spent part of each day reading the classics or current poets. Reading was precious family time. Sofonisba could often be found reading Petrarch's sonnets or Michelangelo's sketchbooks.

EMPRESS CATHERINE THE GREAT (1729–1796): Born into a poor yet noble Prussian family, Princess Sophie grew up in Germany and was neglected because she wasn't a boy. She found refuge in being well educated by her governess. Later she married the Russian tzar Peter the Great (who wasn't so great), and she became known as Catherine the Great. She had an ill-matched, unhappy marriage but escaped her misery by reading. She first read novels and the letters of Madame de Sévigné. Then she read and corresponded with the great philosophical minds of the Enlightenment like Voltaire, Montesquieu, and Diderot. She also read about art, music, history, and more. She even read the dictionary! She read and read; then she ruled. She founded the first national library and the first schools for girls in Russia.

JANE AUSTEN (1775–1817): Jane is famous for her witty novels, now considered classics. She is often cited as an inspiration for other readers. Some of Jane's favorite books—like Carl Grosse's *Horrid Mysteries*—were considered inappropriate, as they were scary and shocking. But Jane read on. Her father gave her the run of his library. By age thirteen she had read a hundred different novels and plays. She bragged in an essay, "You must know, sir, I am a great reader."

MARGARET FULLER (1810–1850): Margaret was a famous journalist and one of the earliest women's rights activists. Her father, educated at Harvard, was determined that his daughter would be "the heir of all he knew." He kept her on a demanding literary diet of the classics. But even at nine, she was sneaking in popular novels like Italian thrillers, German fantasies with fair queens, and romance books. Margaret wasn't allowed to go to Harvard (since she was a woman), but she was so intelligent, so well read, that she became the first woman allowed to use Harvard's library.

ADA LOVELACE (1815–1852): Young Ada, Countess of Lovelace, could usually be found on the lawn with her cat named Puff on her lap, reading some practical tome like William Bingley's *Useful Knowledge*. From a wealthy, noble family, she was superbly educated at home, especially in math, by the best scholars. Her mother forbade her to read novels or poetry, and Ada (usually) obeyed her mother. Ada grew up to be credited as the world's first computer programmer.

CHARLOTTE (1816–1855) AND EMILY BRONTË (1818–1848): Charlotte and Emily lived bleak lives on the bleak moors of England, with no companions except books and the wind. Their eccentric father spent little time with his children, except to frighten them with ghost stories and encourage their wide reading. The bookish sisters made books of their own, writing dozens of tiny, intricate volumes about imaginary kingdoms. In addition to the Bible, some of their favorite books were by Lord Byron, Sir Walter Scott, William Wordsworth, and William Shakespeare. They also found great delight in reading Thomas Bewick's *A History of British Birds*. Charlotte grew up to write *Jane Eyre*, while Emily wrote *Wuthering Heights*, both considered scandalous at the time.

MARIA MITCHELL (1818–1889): Maria was the first professional woman astronomer in the United States and the first American scientist to discover a comet, which was named "Miss Mitchell's Comet." Born to Quaker parents who believed both boys and girls should be educated, Maria was an avid reader. Books were a way for her to be close to her mother, a former librarian. She spent her days reading and her nights studying the sky with her father, an amateur astronomer. By eighteen she had read five giant volumes about celestial mechanics.

LOUISA MAY ALCOTT (1832–1888): Louisa's father taught her the alphabet by having them both lie on the floor and use their legs as "pencils" to draw the letters. Reading was family time, as her father read aloud to her and her three sisters. Louisa started selling her own stories at sixteen, supporting her whole family. Appalled at the current state of children's books, her father urged his daughter to write a really good one. Her response was *Little Women*.

DR. MARIE CURIE (1867–1934): Marie started reading aloud to her older siblings at age four. She decided that science was a way to improve the world, but education for girls in Poland ended at age eighteen. She refused to be deterred. She joined the Floating University, an illegal school where women met in secret. Books would empower her onward. Marie became a world-famous chemist and physicist, winner of two Nobel Prizes, and sharer of books with her two smart daughters.

DR. MARIA MONTESSORI (1870–1952): At twelve years old Maria loved her math and science textbooks so much that she snuck them into theaters and read in the dim light instead of watching the plays with her parents. A big problem she faced was that she didn't want to teach, which was the only career then open to educated women. She persevered and became Italy's first female doctor. She eventually changed her mind about teaching and ended up developing her own theory of education. Today schools all over the world bear her name.

ANNE CARROLL MOORE (1871–1961): Anne loved reading Aesop's fables, Hans Christian Andersen's fairy tales, and bound volumes of *St. Nicholas Magazine* (a popular monthly American children's publication). She spent a lot of time reading at home in Maine. This was because, in her day, children weren't allowed in libraries. Anne thought that was rude. She became a librarian and designed library spaces for children and hired librarians committed to working with young patrons. She became the head of children's services for the New York Public Library. She was also a popular reviewer of children's books and famously kept a NOT RECOMMENDED stamp on her library desk.

GERTRUDE STEIN (1874–1946): Gertrude was an American modernist writer who questioned narrative structures of her time. She pushed for writers and artists to innovate and create their own styles. An avid reader and a host of literary gatherings, she once wrote that she and her brother, Leo, liked to stay home "eating fruit and reading books." She spent all her allowance at secondhand bookstores around Oakland and San Francisco. She bought classic novels, history, and poetry. Escaping an unhappy house, she found refuge in libraries and read just about anything. In the garden with her feet up, she recited poetry, loudly enough to disturb neighbors.

MARY MCLEOD BETHUNE (1875–1955): One day a young Mary was helping her mother at work. She picked up a book in the bedroom of the white people to whom she was delivering laundry. A white child snatched the book away, assuming Mary, who was Black, didn't know how to read. At that moment Mary realized books were one of the things white kids had that Black kids did not. She was determined to be a reader. The first book she loved was the Bible, especially the stories with strong women. She founded training schools to educate Black girls and became one of the most influential Black educators ever.

MARGARET SANGER (1879–1966): Margaret got little attention in her loud, crowded house. Her mother was pregnant eighteen times and died in her late forties. Growing up poor, she read the few books they had, including medical books her father, a stonemason, had used to treat his family. In college she trained to be a nurse. Her well-worn favorite book was a textbook on nursing. Margaret grew up to champion reproductive rights and women's healthcare.

HELEN KELLER (1880–1968): Because Helen was blind and deaf, her early childhood was terribly isolated until she met her teacher, Anne Sullivan. When she learned to read books in Braille—a code of raised dots on a page that allows blind people to read with their fingers—she was suddenly part of the world, going on all kinds of adventures in her mind. As a young reader, she enjoyed reading fables and authors like Shakespeare, Tennyson, and Plato. She also liked Washington Irving's short story "The Legend of Sleepy Hollow." Helen was the first deaf-blind person to earn a bachelor's degree.

ZORA NEALE HURSTON (1891–1960): No one knew her myths like Zora. In the fifth grade, when she was asked to recite the story of Pluto and Persephone, Zora blew everyone away. She loved to read—she read fairy tales, Johann David Wyss's *Swiss Family Robinson*, Jonathan Swift's *Gulliver's Travels*, and best of all, books about mythology. Zora had read hundreds of books by the time she started college. She broke new ground as an African American writer and collector of folklore.

FRIDA KAHLO (1907–1954): Frida's father gave her book after book and fostered her interest in nature. Her happiest hours were spent collecting bugs and plants, taking them home to read about them, and inspecting them under a microscope. By her teens she was reading all the world's classics in three different languages. She loved one book above all: Marcel Schwob's *Imaginary Lives*, which was a collection of dark, edgy stories. She memorized every word. Frida became a renowned painter and one of the most famous Mexican artists of all time. She is most known for her self-portraits.

RACHEL CARSON (1907–1964): Rachel shared the same two passions as her mother: nature and books. Both inspired wonder in her. Her favorite books were about the sea; she loved reading books by Herman Melville, Robert Louis Stevenson, and others. She figured out how to combine her love for nature and books—when she was nine she wrote her own book about animals. Rachel changed the world with her book on environmental science, *Silent Spring*.

URSULA NORDSTROM (1910–1988): As a book editor, Ursula transformed the field of children's literature. She wanted "good books for bad children." She didn't want books that taught about manners or that had morals or lessons. She edited such famous children's books as *Charlotte's Web* by E. B. White, *Goodnight Moon* by Margaret Wise Brown, *Where the Wild Things Are* by Maurice Sendak, *The Giving Tree* by Shel Silverstein, and *Harriet the Spy* by Louise Fitzhugh. As part of the LGBTQ+ community, she supported other LGBTQ+ folks in the industry like Brown, Fitzhugh, and Sendak.

ANNE FRANK (1929–1945): "I'm crazy about reading and books," Anne declared. She read everything from movie magazines and romance novels to Dutch sagas and legends, Greek and Roman myths, and any kind of history book. But the most important book in her life was the red-and-white diary she got for her thirteenth birthday. She named it Kitty, and it was the first thing she packed when, as a German-Dutch Jewish girl, she was forced to go into hiding during the Nazi occupation of the Netherlands in World War II. Anne is the author of the world's most famous diary, which has inspired and informed people all over the world.

FIRST LADY JACQUELINE KENNEDY (1929–1994): Jackie was an inspirational First Lady and later an editor of distinguished books. Before she started school, she read all the children's books in her house. Her heroes included Mowgli from Rudyard Kipling's *The Jungle Book*, Robin Hood, Little Lord Fauntleroy's grandfather created by Frances Hodgson Burnett, and Scarlett O'Hara from Margaret Mitchell's *Gone with the Wind*. She also liked reading Lord Byron's poems. Her beloved grandfather self-published a history of their family that claimed they were descended from French royalty. This wasn't true, but Jackie fell in love with all things French, so she read as much as she could about French history. President John F. Kennedy, who was also an avid reader, wooed Jackie with books.

DOLORES HUERTA (BORN 1930): Dolores is a Mexican American labor leader and civil rights activist. She was a bookish girl whose favorite book might have been the *Girl Scout Handbook*. She was an active member of the Girl Scouts from age six, once winning second prize in the organization's writing contest.

JUDY BLUME (BORN 1938): To Judy, books are like really good friends. She writes honest, humorous stories that address tween and teen issues. As a young girl, she loved reading the Betsy-Tacy books by Maud Hart Lovelace and the Madeline books by Ludwig Bemelmans. Judy loved going to the library to read both adult novels and children's books. Back then she made up stories for her paper dolls; now she makes up stories for millions of readers of all ages.

WILMA MANKILLER (1945–2010): Wilma was the first woman chief of the Cherokee Nation. Her family's move from Oklahoma to San Francisco almost broke ten-year-old Wilma's spirit. It burned when kids made fun of her drawl and her last name. So she and her sister would stay up late every night reading aloud to each other, working hard to master their English. She especially enjoyed reading stories about her native heritage.

FIRST LADY LAURA BUSH (BORN 1946): Before Laura was the First Lady of the United States, she was a shy girl growing up in Texas. She said, "When I was a little girl, my mother would read stories to me. I have loved books and going to the library ever since." She enjoyed reading Laura Ingalls Wilder's Little House books and Louisa May Alcott's *Little Women*. As a young child, she would pretend to teach her dolls how to read and write, holding up picture books to them. Fittingly, she eventually became a public school teacher and librarian.

RUBY BRIDGES (BORN 1954): Ruby has had several books written about her. She became a civil rights activist when she was six years old. She was the first Black child to go to an all-white school in the South, sparking violent protest. Amid crowds so fierce she needed four federal marshals to escort her, she walked in and read on. She learned to read in the first grade. She never forgot the box of Dr. Seuss books sent by an anonymous supporter. It was a box full of silliness that helped her during a nightmarish time in her personal life and in our nation's history.

MAYA LIN (BORN 1959): Maya is an Asian American architect and sculptor. Her parents were working professionals, so Maya learned to keep herself busy throughout her childhood in Ohio. She built miniature towns, hiked, watched birds, and read. She was fascinated with the natural world and with science. She liked to read books about these topics. She also devoured fantasy books like J. R. R. Tolkien's *The Hobbit*. Fantasy books freed her imagination, and she used it in all kinds of ways, especially when she was experimenting with art. She grew up to design the Vietnam Veterans Memorial in Washington, D.C., at age twenty-one.

FIRST LADY MICHELLE OBAMA (BORN 1964): Michelle learned to read by age four. When she went to school, Michelle felt "confident" in her ability to read since she had plowed through the Dick and Jane books. As a young reader, her favorite character was a "strong little girl" named Pippi Longstocking, created by Astrid Lindgren. Michelle credits her mother with teaching her how to read. Her mother walked Michelle to the public library in their hometown of Chicago. She sat with Michelle as she sounded out words. To this day, Michelle still enjoys reading aloud. She fondly recalls reading aloud to her own daughters, passing on to them the love of reading. As a family, Michelle and her daughters, Sasha and Malia, read all seven of J. K. Rowling's Harry Potter books aloud, even with their very busy dad, President Barack Obama.

ACTIVITIES TO KEEP READING

Do you love to read? Are you inspired to read on? Be a part of the book-loving community. Engage in these bookish activities and spread the joy of reading:

- **KEEP A READING JOURNAL**: Get a notebook and track your reading. List the author and book title, the date you started reading it, the date you finished reading it, and a few comments. Make notes about your favorite characters, quotes, and so forth. Consider creating a rating system.

- **COORDINATE A BOOK CLUB**: Read books and host discussion groups to talk about the books you have read. These are great opportunities for people to get together (either virtually or in person) and learn new things. Remember to send out invitations, create discussion questions, and share snacks! The best part of being in a book club is choosing the books to read. Make sure to agree with members on how books get selected.

- **HOST A BOOK DRIVE**: Collect new and gently used books. Ask friends, family, and community members to send books to you. Make sure you have a place to store the books. Then donate the books to communities that need them, such as schools, classrooms, after-school programs, childcare centers, prisons, or migrant work camps.

- **VOLUNTEER TO READ ALOUD**: Practice your reading skills and keep others company by sharing stories. Read aloud at a senior citizens' home. Or read aloud to a younger sibling or a student in a younger grade. You can even read aloud to dogs being housed at animal shelters.

RESOURCES

HOW TO ACCESS FREE BOOKS

- **PUBLIC LIBRARIES**: Libraries hold collections of books, videos, and more. They lend them out to community members. They also host programs. They're free and open to the public. Make sure you sign up for a library card!
- **LITTLE FREE LIBRARIES**: Some houses and businesses have free book-sharing boxes outside their buildings. They allow neighbors to take and share books.
- **ONLINE LIBRARIES**: There are several resources online that allow young readers to access books for free. For example, the International Children's Digital Library (http://www.childrenslibrary.org/index.html) is an online collection of children's books from around the world.

ORGANIZATIONS THAT HELP GIRLS TO READ

#1000BLACKGIRLBOOKS

marleydias.com/1000blackgirlbooks/

Marley Dias started this campaign to promote the reading of more books with Black girls as the main characters. This website provides a database of resources and a way to donate books to underserved communities.

CAMPAIGN FOR FEMALE EDUCATION (CAMFED)

camfed.org/us/

CAMFED's mission is to eradicate poverty in Africa by educating and empowering young women. It supports girls who are denied access to education by paying for their school costs.

CARE: EDUCATION

care.org/our-work/education-and-work/education/

CARE works to increase access to quality education for marginalized children, especially teen girls living in fragile and conflict-affected settings. Programs include the Somali Girls' Education Promotion Programme–Transition, the Patsy Collins Trust Fund Initiative, Azraq Film School, and Strengthening Opportunities for Adolescent Resilience (SOAR).

GIRL RISING

girlrising.org

Girl Rising is a global campaign for girls' education and empowerment. It uses storytelling, such as feature films and other media tools, to change the way the world values women and to break down barriers to girls' education.

GIRL UP

girlup.org/issues/education

Girl Up is a campaign for girls, by girls. It encourages American girls to raise awareness and funds for girls in the developing world. It works with a network of United Nations partners to ensure that teen girls around the world have access to education.

HARPSWELL FOUNDATION

harpswellfoundation.org

The Harpswell Foundation strives to educate young women in Southeast Asia so that they can become leaders for social and economic change. The foundation manages educational centers in Cambodia and Malaysia.

MALALA FUND

malala.org

Malala Yousafzai established this organization with the sole purpose of working for a world in which every girl can learn and lead. The Malala Fund invests in education activists and advocates who are driving solutions to barriers to girls' education in their communities.

SHE'S THE FIRST

shesthefirst.org

She's the First fights gender inequality through education by providing scholarships and support. The organization started as a social media campaign centered on a YouTube video featuring the singer JoJo.

ORGANIZATIONS THAT HELP CHILDREN TO READ

BOOK AID INTERNATIONAL

bookaid.org

Book Aid International provides books and supports libraries in Africa and around the world. It sends books to prisons, refugee camps, hospitals, schools, and elsewhere.

CAMBODIAN CHILDREN'S FUND

cambodianchildrensfund.org/how-we-work/education

The Cambodian Children's Fund strives to improve the lives of the poorest children in Phnom Penh, Cambodia. It provides educational opportunities and scholarships for Cambodia's orphaned and vulnerable children.

DOLLY PARTON'S IMAGINATION LIBRARY

imaginationlibrary.com

Dolly Parton's project is dedicated to inspiring a love of reading by gifting books, free of charge, to children from birth to age five. Dolly was inspired by her father's inability to read and write. Her library started in her home county and now expands into countries all around the world.

FIRST BOOK

firstbook.org

First Book believes that education is the best way out of poverty for children in need. It provides books and other resources.

MAGIC BUS

magicbus.org

Magic Bus hosts a "Childhood to Livelihood" program that enables children to complete a secondary education in order to attain employable skills. It aims to break cycles of poverty in South Asia.

NEPAL YOUTH FOUNDATION

nepalyouthfoundation.org

Nepal Youth Foundation is a U.S.-based organization that works to provide Nepal's most impoverished children with an education and other freedoms.

OPRAH FOUNDATION: EDUCATION

oprahfoundation.org/eduation

Oprah Winfrey has contributed millions of dollars in scholarships and various educational endeavors. She is committed to providing underserved communities access to quality education.

REACH OUT AND READ

reachoutandread.org

Reach Out and Read works directly with children's doctors to promote early literacy. It encourages families to read aloud to their children every day.

READING IS FUNDAMENTAL

rif.org

Reading Is Fundamental is committed to promoting a literate America, believing that every child deserves opportunities to own books and learn how to read. It gives out books, provides reading resources, and hosts supplemental reading programs.

ROOM TO READ

roomtoread.org

Room to Read strives to improve literacy and gender equality in education in the developing world. It believes that "world change starts with educated children." It develops literacy skills and the habits of reading among primary school children and supports girls in completing secondary school.

UNITED THROUGH READING

unitedthroughreading.org

United Through Reading connects military families who are separated by providing the bonding experience of shared story time.

REFERENCES*

INTRODUCTION

Badia, Janet, and Jennifer Phegley, eds. *Reading Women: Literary Figures and Cultural Icons from the Victorian Age to the Present.* Toronto, Canada: University of Toronto Press, 2005.

Castagna, Edwin. *Caught in the Act: The Decisive Reading of Some Notable Men and Women and Its Influence on Their Thoughts and Actions.* Metuchen, NJ: Scarecrow Press, 1982.

Claybourne, Anna. *Ancient Greece.* Chicago: Raintree Publishing, 2007.

Crain, Patricia. *Reading Children: Literacy, Property, and the Dilemmas of Childhood in Nineteenth-Century America.* Philadelphia: University of Pennsylvania Press, 2017.

Fischer, Steven Roger. *A History of Reading.* London: Reaktion Books, 2003.

Flint, Kate. *The Woman Reader, 1837–1914.* New York: Oxford University Press, 1993.

Green, D. H. *Women Readers in the Middle Ages.* Cambridge: Cambridge University Press, 2007.

Harris, Michael H. *History of Libraries in the Western World.* Metuchen, NJ: Scarecrow Press, 1995.

Hill, Catey. "How Donald Trump and #MeToo Are Shaking Up the Children's Book Market." *Market Watch*, September 11, 2018. https://www.marketwatch.com/story/how-donald-trump -and-metoo-are-shaking-up-the-childrens-book-market-2018-09-11.

Jack, Belinda. *The Woman Reader.* New Haven, CT: Yale University Press, 2012.

Kristof, Nicholas. "Graduate of the Year." *New York Times*, May 24, 2014.

Kristof, Nicolas, and Sheryl Wudunn. *Half the Sky: Turning Oppression into Opportunity for Women Worldwide.* New York: Knopf, 2009.

Manguel, Alberto. *A History of Reading.* New York: Viking Penguin, 1996.

Mavrody, Nika. "The Dangers of Reading in Bed." *The Atlantic*, May 19, 2017. https://www.theatlantic.com/technology/archive/2017/05/reading-in-bed/527388/.

McGraw, Eliza. "Horse-Riding Librarians Were the Great Depression's Bookmobiles." *Smithsonian Magazine*, June 21, 2017. https://www.smithsonianmag.com/history/horse-riding -librarians-were-great-depression-bookmobiles-180963786/.

*All online sources listed here accessed between October 2021 and March 2022.

Price, Leah. *What We Talk about When We Talk about Books: The History and Future of Reading*. New York: Basic Books, 2019.

Rosenberg, Rosalind. *Beyond Separate Spheres: Intellectual Roots of Modern Feminism*. New Haven, CT: Yale University Press, 1982.

Vincent, David. *The Rise of Mass Literacy: Reading and Writing in Modern Europe*. Malden, MA: Blackwell, 2000.

Willes, Margaret. *Reading Matters: Five Centuries of Discovering Books*. New Haven, CT: Yale University Press, 2008.

CLEOPATRA

Chauveau, Michael. *Cleopatra: Beyond the Myth*. Ithaca, NY: Cornell University Press, 2004.

Crawford, Amy. "Who Was Cleopatra? Mythology, Propaganda, Liz Taylor, and the Real Queen of the Nile." *Smithsonian Magazine*, March 31, 2007. https://www.smithsonianmag.com /history/who-was-cleopatra-151356013/.

El Daly, Okasha. *Egyptology: The Missing Millennium: Ancient Egypt in Medieval Arabic Writings*. London: Routledge, 2008.

Krull, Kathleen. *Lives of Extraordinary Women: Rulers, Rebels (and What the Neighbors Thought)*. Boston: HMH Books for Young Readers, 2013.

Pelling, Christopher, ed. *Plutarch: Life of Antony*. Cambridge, England: Cambridge University Press, 1988.

Schiff, Stacy. *Cleopatra: A Life*. New York: Little, Brown and Company, 2010.

Shakespeare, William. *Antony and Cleopatra*. New York: W. W. Norton & Company, 2011.

Shecter, Vicky Alvear. *Cleopatra Rules! The Amazing Life of the Original Teen Queen*. Honesdale, PA: Boyds Mills Press, 2010.

Thurman, Judith. "The Cleopatriad." *New Yorker*, November 15, 2010. https://www.newyorker .com/magazine/2010/11/15/the-cleopatriad.

WU ZETIAN

Anderson, Mary. *Hidden Power: The Palace Eunuchs of Imperial China*. Amherst, MA: Prometheus Books, 1990.

Barrett, T. H. *The Woman Who Discovered Printing*. New Haven, CT: Yale University Press, 2008.

Chang, Kang-I Sun, Huan Saussy, and Charles Yim-tze Kwong. *Women Writers of Traditional China:*

An Anthology of Poetry and Criticism. Redwood City, CA: Stanford University Press, 2000.

Clements, Jonathan. *Wu: The Chinese Empress Who Schemed, Seduced, and Murdered Her Way to Become a Living God.* Stroud, United Kingdom: Sutton Publishing, 2007.

Dash, Mike. "The Demonization of Empress Wu." *Smithsonian Magazine*, August 10, 2012. https://www.smithsonianmag.com/history/the-demonization-of-empress-wu-20743091/.

Halligan, Katherine. *Herstory: 50 Women and Girls Who Shook Up the World.* New York: Simon & Schuster Books for Young Readers, 2018.

Lee, Yuen Ting. "Wu Zhao: Ruler of Tang Dynasty China." *Education about Asia 20*, no. 2 (Fall 2015). https://www.asianstudies.org/wp-content/uploads/wu-zhao-ruler-of-tang-dynasty-china.pdf.

Rothschild, N. Harry. *Wu Zhao: China's Only Woman Emperor.* New York: Pearson, 2008.

Stone, Charles. *The Fountainhead of Chinese Erotica: The Lord of Perfect Satisfaction.* Honolulu: University of Hawai'i Press, 2003.

Twitchett, Denis C., ed. *The Cambridge History of China.* Vol. 3, *Sui and T'ang China*, 589–906, pt. I, pp. 244–245. Cambridge: Cambridge University Press, 1979.

Workers Theoretical Group of Qinghua University Kindergarten. "Several Opinions on Wu Zetian." *Beijing University Journal*, no. 4 (1974).

Yang, Lian Sheng. "Female Rulers in Imperial China." *Harvard Journal of Asiatic Studies 23* (1960–1961): 47–61.

QUEEN ELIZABETH I

Creighton, Mandell. *Queen Elizabeth.* Princeton, NJ: Longmans, Green and Company, 1920.

Friedman, Alice. T. "The Influence of Humanism on the Education of Girls and Boys in Tudor England." *History of Education Quarterly 25*, no. 1–2 (Spring–Summer 1985): 57–70.

Haugaard, William. P. "Elizabeth Tudor's 'Book of Devotions': A Neglected Clue to the Queen's Life and Character." *Sixteenth Century Journal 12*, no. 2 (1981): 79–106.

Hibbert, Christopher. *The Virgin Queen: Elizabeth I, Genius of the Golden Age.* Boston: Da Capo Press, 1991.

Krull, Kathleen. *Lives of Extraordinary Women: Rulers, Rebels (and What the Neighbors Thought).* Boston: HMH Books for Young Readers, 2013.

Levine, Carole. *The Heart and Stomach of a King: Elizabeth I and the Politics of Sex and Power.* Philadelphia: University of Pennsylvania Press, 1994.

Lewis, Jone Johnson. "Queen Elizabeth I Quotes." *ThoughtCo.*, February 2, 2019. https://www.thoughtco.com/queen-elizabeth-i-quotes-3530018.

Marcus, Leah S., Janel Mueller, and Mary Beth Rose, eds. *Elizabeth I: Collected Works*. Chicago: University of Chicago Press, 2000.

McCain, John, and Mark Salter. *Character Is Destiny: Inspiring Stories Every Young Person Should Know and Every Adult Should Remember*. New York: Random House, 2005.

Nicolas, Lucy R. *Roger Ascham and His Sixteenth-Century World*. Leiden, Netherlands: Brill Publishers, 2020.

Norton, Elizabeth. *The Hidden Lives of Tudor Women: A Social History*. New York: Pegasus Books, 2017.

Plowden, Alison. *The Young Elizabeth*. New York: Macmillan Publishers, 2002.

Starkey, David. *Elizabeth: The Struggle for the Throne*. New York: HarperCollins, 2000.

Starkey, David. *Six Wives: The Queens of Henry VIII*. New York: Harper Perennial, 2003.

Weir, Alison. *Children of England: The Heirs of Henry VIII*. New York: Ballantine Books, 1996.

SOR (SISTER) JUANA INÉS DE LA CRUZ

Academy of American Poets. "Sor Juana Inés de la Cruz." Poets.org. https://poets.org/poet/sor-juana-ines-de-la-cruz.

Cruz, Juana Ines de la. *Sor Juana Inés de la Cruz: Selected Works*. New York: W. W. Norton & Company, 2014.

Cruz, Juana Ines de la. *A Woman of Genius: The Intellectual Biography of Sor Juana Inés de la Cruz*. Salisbury, CT: Lime Rock Press, 1982.

Grossman-Heinze, Dahia. "My Favorite Feminist: Sor Juana Inés de la Cruz." *Ms. Magazine*, March 16, 2011. https://msmagazine.com/2011/03/16/my-favorite-feminist-sor-juana-ines-de-la-cruz/.

Mora, Pat. *A Library for Juana: The World of Sor Juana Inés*. New York: Knopf, 2002.

National Endowment for the Humanities. "The Poetic Nun." NEH.gov, January 20, 2012. https://www.neh.gov/news/the-poetic-nun.

Paz, Octavio. *Sor Juana: Or, The Traps of Faith*. Cambridge, MA: Belknap Press, 1988.

Prager, Sarah. *Queer, There, and Everywhere: 23 People Who Changed the World*. New York: HarperCollins, 2017.

Ritchie, Joy, and Kate Ronald, eds. *Available Means: An Anthology of Women's Rhetoric*. Pittsburgh, PA: University of Pittsburgh Press, 2001.

"Sor Juana (1648–1695)." Project Vox, Duke University Libraries. https://projectvox.org/sor-juana-1648-1695/.

"Sor Juana Inés de la Cruz." Biography, April 1, 2014. https://www.biography.com/writer/sor-juana-ines-de-la-cruz.

Tariq, Aima. "The Miserable Life of the Feminist Nun." Lessons from History, March 11, 2021. https://medium.com/lessons-from-history/the-miserable-life-of-the-feminist-nun-f3d88b19ac14.

PHILLIS WHEATLEY PETERS

Bennett, Lerone. *Before the Mayflower: A History of Black America*. Chicago: Johnson Publishing Company, 1993.

Boston African American National Historic Site. "Phillis Wheatley's Journey." National Park Service. https://www.nps.gov/articles/phillis-wheatleys-journey.htm.

Carretta, Vincent. *Phillis Wheatley: Biography of a Genius in Bondage*. Athens: University of Georgia Press, 2011.

Carretta, Vincent, ed. *Phillis Wheatley: Complete Writings*. New York: Penguin Books, 2001.

Cooper, Afua. *My Name Is Phillis Wheatley: A Story of Slavery and Freedom*. Toronto, Canada: Kids Can Press, 2009.

Gates, Jr., Henry Louis. *The Trials of Phillis Wheatley: America's First Black Poet and Her Encounters with the Founding Fathers*. New York: Basic Civitas Books, 2010.

Michals, Debra, ed. "Phillis Wheatley." National Women's History Museum, 2015. https://www.womenshistory.org/education-resources/biographies/phillis-wheatley.

O'Neale, Sondra A. "Phillis Wheatley." Poetry Foundation. https://www.poetryfoundation.org/poets/phillis-wheatley.

Perkins, Douglas. "General Washington Welcomes an Honored Guest." *History of Yesterday*, January 13, 2021. https://historyofyesterday.com/general-washington-welcomes-an-honored-guest-3bdb76ddaf1b.

Winkler, Elizabeth. "How Phillis Wheatley Was Recovered through History." *New Yorker*, July 30, 2020. https://www.newyorker.com/booksunder-review-how-phillis-wheatley-was-recovered-through-history.

E. PAULINE JOHNSON

Boag, Veronica, and Carole Gerson. *Paddling Her Own Canoe: The Times and Texts of E. Pauline Johnson (Tekahionwake)*. Toronto, Canada: University of Toronto Press, 2000.

"Emily Pauline Johnson." Poetry Foundation. https://www.poetryfoundation.org/poets/emily-pauline-johnson.

Fee, Margery, and Dory Naso, eds. *Tekahionwake: E. Pauline Johnson's Writings on Native North America*. Ontario, Canada: Broadview Press, 2015.

Garvin, John William, ed. *Canadian Poets*. Toronto, Canada: McClelland, Goodchild & Steward Publishers, 1916.

Gray, Charlotte. "The Complicated Case of Pauline Johnson." *The Walrus*, October 23, 2019. https://thewalrus.ca/the-complicated-case-of-pauline-johnson/.

Gray, Charlotte. *Flint & Feather: The Life and Times of E. Pauline Johnson*. Toronto, Canada: Harper Flamingo, 2002.

Gray, Charlotte. "The True Story of Pauline Johnson: Poet, Provocateur, and Champion of Indigenous Rights." *Canadian Geographic*, March 8, 2017. https://www.canadiangeographic .ca/article/true-story-pauline-johnson-poet-provocateur-and-champion indigenous-rights.

Jackel, David. "Johnson, Pauline." *The Oxford Companion to Canadian Literature*, edited by W. Toye. Toronto, Canada: Oxford University Press, 1983.

Johnson, E. Pauline. *Collected Poems and Selected Prose*. Toronto, Canada: University of Toronto Press.

Robinson, Amanda. "Pauline Johnson (Tekahionwake)." *Canadian Encyclopedia*, April 14, 2008. https://www.thecanadianencyclopedia.ca/en/article/pauline-johnson.

Swenson, Jeffrey. "A Scrap of the Savage: E. Pauline Johnson's Canoeing Journalism." *Studies in Canadian Literature/Études en Littérature Canadienne* 43, no. 1 (2018): 69–90. https:// journals.lib.unb.ca/index.php/SCL/article/view/28793/1882521601.

CHIEN-SHIUNG WU

American Association of University Women. "Chien-Shiung Wu Overlooked for Nobel Prize." AAUW.org. https://www.aauw.org/resources /faces-of-aauwchien-shiung-wu-overlooked-for-nobel-prize/.

Chiang, Tsai-Chien. *Madame Wu Chien-Shiung: The First Lady of Physics Research*. Singapore: World Scientific, 2014.

Lough, René. "Universe in Reverse: The Queen of Physics Chien-Shiung Wu." Medium.com, April 20, 2018. https://lough-and-behold.medium.comuniverse-in-reverse-the-queen-of-physics -chien-shiung-wu-1ba8f6b3cfff.

Lucibella, Michael. "Women and the Nobel Prize in Physics." *APS News* 22, no. 11 (December 2013). https://www.aps.org/publications/apsnews/201312/physicshistory.cfm.

McGrayne, Sharon Bertsch. *Nobel Prize Women in Science: Their Lives, Struggles, and*

Momentous Discoveries. Washington, D.C.: Joseph Henry Press, 1998.

Smeltzer, Ronald K. "Chien-Shiung Wu." Atomic Heritage Foundation. https://www
.atomicheritage.org/profile/chien-shiung-wu.

Worthen, Meredith. "Chien-Shiung Wu." Biography, June 1, 2016. https://www.biography
.com/scientist/chien-shiung-wu.

Yuan, Jada. "Discovering Dr. Wu." *Washington Post*, December 13, 2021. https://www
.washingtonpost.com/lifestyle/2021/12/13/chien-shiung-wu-biography-physics-grandmother/.

INDIRA GANDHI

Frank, Katherine. *Indira: The Life of Indira Nehru Gandhi*. New York: HarperCollins, 2010.

Gandhi, Indira. *Selected Speeches of Indira Gandhi: January 1, 1982–October 30, 1984*.
Publications Division, Ministry of Information and Broadcasting, Government of India, 1986.

Gandhi, Indira. "What Educated Women Can Do." Speech at the Golden Jubilee Celebrations of the
Indraprastha College for Women in New Delhi, India, 1974. http://www.edchange.org/multicultural
/speeches/indira_gandhi_educated.html.

Genovese, Michael A., ed. *Women as National Leaders*. Newbury Park, CA: Sage Publications,
1993.

Gupte, Pranay. *Mother India: A Political Biography of Indira Gandhi*. New York: Penguin Books,
2011.

Halligan, Katherine. *Herstory: 50 Women and Girls Who Shook Up the World*. New York: Simon
& Schuster Books for Young Readers, 2018.

Jayakar, Pupul. *Indira Gandhi: A Biography*. New York: Penguin Group, 1997.

Krull, Kathleen. *Lives of Extraordinary Women: Rulers, Rebels (and What the Neighbors
Thought)*. Boston: HMH Books for Young Readers, 2013.

Norman, Dorothy. *Indira Gandhi: Letters to an American Friend*. San Diego: Harcourt Brace
Jovanovich, 1985.

Ramesh, Jairam. *Indira Gandhi: A Life in Nature*. New York: Simon & Schuster, 2019.

Somervil, Barbara A. *Indira Gandhi: Political Leader in India*. Minneapolis, MN: Compass Point
Books, 2007.

REFERENCES

SHIRLEY CHISHOLM

Brownmiller, Susan. *Shirley Chisholm: A Biography*. New York: Doubleday & Company, 1971.

Chisholm, Shirley. "The 51% Minority." Address delivered at the Conference on Women's Employment, sponsored by the National Organization for Women, Chicago, January 24, 1970. https://repositories.lib.utexas.edu/handle/2152/12894.

Chisholm, Shirley. *The Good Fight*. New York: HarperCollins, 1973.

Chisholm, Shirley. *Unbought and Unbossed*. New York: Houghton Mifflin, 1970.

History, Art & Archives, United States House of Representatives. "Chisholm, Shirley Anita." https://history.house.gov/People/Listing/C/CHISHOLM,-Shirley-Anita-(C000371)/.

Lesher, Stephan. "The Short, Unhappy Life of Black Presidential Politics, 1972." *New York Times Magazine*, June 25, 1972. https://www.nytimes.com/1972/06/25/archives/the-short-unhappy-life-of-black-presidential-politics-1972-black.html.

Michals, Debra. "Shirley Chisholm." National Women's History Museum, 2015. https://www.womenshistory.org/education-resources/biographies/shirley-chisholm.

Raatma, Lucia. *Shirley Chisholm*. New York: Marshall Cavendish, 2011.

Winslow, Barbara. *Shirley Chisholm: Catalyst for Change*. New York: Routledge, 2019.

PATSY MINK

Alexander, Kerri Lee. "Patsy Mink." National Women's History Museum, 2019. https://www.womenshistory.org/education-resources/biographies/patsy-mink.

Arinaga, Esther K., and Rene E. Ojiri. "Patsy Takemoto Mink." *Asian-Pacific Law & Policy Journal* 4, no. 2 (2003): 571–597.

Cooper, Ilene. *A Woman in the House (and Senate): How Women Came to Washington and Changed the Nation*. New York: Harry N. Abrams, 2020.

Davidson, Sue. *A Heart in Politics: Jeannette Rankin and Patsy T. Mink*. New York: Seal Press, 1994.

Lee, Ellen. "Patsy Takemoto Mink's Trailblazing Testimony against a Supreme Court Nominee." *The Atlantic*, September 16, 2018. https://www.theatlantic.com/politics/archive/2018/09/patsy-takemoto-minks-trailblazing-testimony-against-a-supreme-court-nominee/570082/.

Loh-Hagan, Virginia. *Patsy Mink*. Ann Arbor, MI: Cherry Lake Publishing, 2021.

Louie, Ai-Ling. *Patsy Mink, Mother of Title 9*. Bethesda, MD: Dragoneagle Press, 2018.

Wu, Judy Tzu-Chun. "Asian American Feminisms and Legislative Activism: Patsy Takemoto Mink in the U.S. Congress." In *Our Voices, Our Histories: Asian American and Pacific Islander Women*, edited by Shirley Hune and Gail M. Nomura, pp. 304–320. New York: New York University Press, 2020.

Wu, Judy Tze-Chun, and Gwendolyn Mink. *Fierce and Fearless: Patsy Takemoto Mink, First Woman of Color in Congress*. New York: New York University Press, 2022.

AUDRE LORDE

"Audre Lorde." Biography, February 18, 2021. https://www.biography.com/writer/audre-lorde.

"Audre Lorde." Poetry Foundation. https://www.poetryfoundation.org/poets/audre-lorde.

Brandman, Mariana. "Audre Lorde." National Women's History Museum, 2021. https://www.womenshistory.org/education-resources/biographies/audre-lorde.

Hall, Joan Wylie, ed. *Conversations with Audre Lorde*. Jackson: University Press of Mississippi, 2004.

Leonard, Keith D. "'Which Me Will Survive': Rethinking Identity, Reclaiming Audre Lorde." Callaloo 35, no. 3 (Summer 2012): 758–777.

Lorde, Audre. *Zami: A New Spelling of My Name*. New York: Crossing Press, 1962.

Tate, Claudia. *Black Women Writers at Work*. Ann Arbor: University of Michigan, 1983.

Yetunde, Pamela Ayo. "Audre Lorde's Hopelessness and Hopefulness: Cultivating a Womanist Nondualism for Psycho-Spiritual Wholeness." *Feminist Theology* 27, no. 2 (2019): 176–194.

TEMPLE GRANDIN

Demuth, Patricia Brennan. *Who Is Temple Grandin?* New York: Penguin Workshop, 2020.

Donvan, John, and Caren Zuker. "The Early History of Autism in America." *Smithsonian Magazine*, January 2016. https://www.smithsonianmag.com/science-nature/early-history-autism-america-180957684/.

Grandin, Temple. *Thinking in Pictures: My Life with Autism*. New York: Vintage, 2006.

Grandin, Temple. Video for American Library Association. https://www.youtube.com/watch?v=CUSOkBN8dIE.

Grandin, Temple. *The Way I See It: A Personal Look at Autism & Asperger's*. Arlington, TX: Future Horizons, 2008.

Grandin, Temple. Website: http://www.templegrandin.com/.

Sacks, Oliver. "An Anthropologist on Mars." *New Yorker*, December 27, 1993. https://www.newyorker.com/magazine/1993/12/27/anthropologist-mars.

REFERENCES

Simonini, Ross. "An Interview with Temple Grandin." *The Believer*, February 1, 2019. https://thebeliever.net/an-interview-with-temple-grandin/.

Smith, Jen Rose. "Why Temple Grandin Wants Your Kids to Go Outside." CNN, April 19, 2021. https://www.cnn.com/2021/04/19/health/outdoor-science-temple-grandin-scn-wellness/index.html.

SALLY RIDE

Abawi, Atia. *Sally Ride*. New York: Philomel Books, 2021.

Akpan, Nsikan. "The Life of Sally Ride, America's First Woman Astronaut, in Pictures." PBS NewsHour, October 14, 2015. https://www.pbs.org/newshour/science/life-sally-ride-americas-first-woman-astronaut-pictures.

Boyle, Alan. "Why Sally Ride Waited Until Her Death to Tell the World She Was Gay." NBC News, July 24, 2012. https://www.nbcnews.com/sciencemain/why-sally-ride-waited-until-her-death-tell-world-she-908942.

Eisenband, Jeff. "Pioneering Astronaut Sally Ride Almost Opted for Tennis." *Post Game*, July 23, 2012. http://www.thepostgame.com/blog/throwback/201207/pioneering-astronaut-sally-ride-almost-opted-tennis.

Grady, Denise. "American Woman Who Shattered Space Ceiling." *New York Times*, July 24, 2012. https://www.nytimes.com/2012/07/24/science/space/sally-ride-trailblazing-astronaut-dies-at-61.html.

King, Margaret. "20 Things You Might Not Know About Sally Ride." UC San Diego News Center, February 18, 2021. https://ucsdnews.ucsd.edu/feature/20-things-you-might-not-know-about-sally-ride.

Ogle-Mater, Janet. "Sally Ride: The First American Woman in Space." ThougthtCo., January 22, 2020. https://www.thoughtco.com/sally-ride-1779837.

Peralta, Eyder. "Sally Ride, First American Woman in Space, Is Dead." National Public Radio, July 23, 2012. https://www.npr.org/sections/thetwo-way/2012/07/23/157250870/sally-ride-first-american-woman-in-space-is-dead.

Sally Ride Science at UC San Diego. Website: https://sallyridescience.ucsd.edu/about/.

Sherr, Lynn. *Sally Ride: America's First Woman in Space*. New York: Simon & Schuster, 2014.

Stine, Megan. *Who Was Sally Ride?* New York: Penguin Group, 2013.

OPRAH WINFREY

Cooper, Ilene. *Up Close: Oprah Winfrey*. New York: Puffin Books, 2007.

Farr, Cecilia Konchar. *Reading Oprah: How Oprah's Book Club Changed the Way America Reads*. Albany: State University of New York Press, 2004.

Fuller, Danielle, and DeNel Rehberg Sedo. *Reading Beyond the Book: The Social Practices of Contemporary Literary Culture*. New York: Routledge, 2013.

Ganchrow, Banji. "Oprah Winfrey's Greatest Accomplishments." *Longevity*, 2015. https://vocal .media/longevity/oprah-winfreys-greatest-accomplishments.

Kelly, Kitty. *Oprah*. New York: Crown Publishers, 2010.

Kniffel, Leonard. "Reading for Life: Oprah Winfrey." *American Libraries Magazine*, May 25, 2011. https://americanlibrariesmagazinc.org/2011/05/25/reading-for-life-oprah-winfrey/.

Kramer, Barbara. *Who Is Oprah Winfrey?* New York: Penguin Books, 2019.

Krohn, Katherine. *Oprah Winfrey: Global Media Leader*. USA Today Lifeline Biographies. Minneapolis, MN: Twenty-First Century Books, 2009.

Nagle, Jeanne. Oprah Winfrey: Profile of a Media Mogul. New York: Rosen Publishing Group, 2008.

Rose, M. J. "(Book Clubs') Life After Oprah." *Wired*, April 9, 2002. https://www.wired.com /2002/04/book-clubs-life-after-oprah/.

Szalai, Jennifer. "Oprah Winfrey, Book Critic." *New Yorker*, April 24, 2013. https://www .newyorker.com/books/page-turner/oprah-winfrey-book-critic.

Vivinetto, Gina. "Oprah Opens Up to Hoda Kotb about How Her Childhood Trauma Informed Her Life's Work." *Today*, May 21, 2021. https://www.today.com/popculture /oprah-opens-hoda-kotb-about-how-her-childhood-trauma-informed-t219209.

Winfrey, Oprah. "What Oprah Knows for Sure about the Joy of Reading." Oprah.com. https:// www.oprah.com/inspiration/oprah-on-the-joy-of-reading.

SONIA SOTOMAYOR

Angelucci, Ashley. "Sonia Sotomayor." National Women's History Museum, 2021. https://www .womenshistory.org/education-resources/biographies/sonia-sotomayor.

Guadalupe, Patricia. "The Key to Supreme Court Justice Sonia Sotomayor's Successful Journey? It's Books, She Says." NBS News, September 1, 2018. https://www.nbcnews.com/news /latino/key-supreme-court-justice-sonia-sotomayor-s-successful-journey-it-n905536.

Krull, Kathleen. *Women Who Broke the Rules: Sonia Sotomayor*. New York: Bloomsbury, 2015.

Sotomayor, Sonia. *My Beloved World*. New York: Vintage Books, 2013.

Stump, Scott. "Sonia Sotomayor Opens Up about Childhood of 'Neglect.'" *Today*, January 15, 2013. https://www.today.com/news/sonia-sotomayor-opens-about-childhood-neglect -flna1B7976029.

Totenberg, Nina. "A Justice Deliberates: Sotomayor on Love, Health, and Family." National Public Radio, January 12, 2013. https://www.npr.org/2013/01/14/167699633/a-justice -deliberates-sotomayor-on-love-health-and-family.

Vincenty, Samantha. "8 Things You Didn't Know About Supreme Court Justice Sonia Sotomayor." *Oprah Daily*, January 20, 2021. https://www.oprahdaily.com/entertainment/a35256242 /justice-sonia-sotomayor-facts/.

SERENA WILLIAMS

Barshad, Amos. "11 Things We Learned about Serena Williams from Her FADER Cover Story." *Fader*, October 4, 2016. https://www.thefader.com/2016/10/04/serena-williams-fader -interview-facts.

Corbett, Merlisa Lawrence. *Serena Williams: Tennis Champion, Sports Legend, and Cultural Heroine*. New York: Rowman & Littlefield, 2020.

Edmondson, Jacqueline. *Venus and Serena Williams: A Biography*. Westport, CT: Greenwood Press, 2005.

Eichenholz, Andrew. "How Serena Williams Is Using Her Star Power for Good." *Rolling Stone*, July 11, 2016. https://www.rollingstone.com/culture/culture-sports/how-serena-williams-is-using -her-star-power-for-good-223644/.

Grant, Jasmine. "Serena Williams Speaks French with Her 2-Year-Old in This Adorable Video." *Essence*, December 6, 2020. https://www.essence.com/love/ serena-williams-teaches-olympia-french/.

Krull, Kathleen. *Frenemies in the Families: Famous Brothers and Sisters Who Butted Heads and Had Each Other's Backs*. New York: Crown Books, 2018.

Perez, Olivia. "Serena Williams on 'King Richard' and the Entrepreneurial Lessons She Learned from Her Dad." *Forbes*, December 3, 2021. https://www.forbes.com/sites /oliviaperez/2021/12/03/serena-williams-on-family-traditions-king-richard-and-the -entrepreneurial-lessons-she-carries-from-her-dad/?sh=152ab09040fb.

Ritholtz, Barry. "MiB: Serena Williams, Tennis Great." *Big Picture*, March 30, 2018. https://ritholtz.com/2018/03/mib-serena-williams-tennis-great/.

Rosenberg, Eli, and Cindy Boren. "'You're Hastening the Hell You Wish to Avoid': Controversial American Delivers a Shot and Is Called Out by Serena Williams." *Washington Post*, January 24, 2018. https://www.washingtonpost.com/news/early-lead/wp/2018/01/22/meet-americas-new-tennis-sensation-tennys-sandgren-he-should-never-have-tweeted/.

"Serena's Family Photos." *The Guardian*, August 28, 2009. https://www.theguardian.com/sport/gallery/2009/aug/29/serena-williams-tennis.

"Serena Williams — Rise." Goalcast. https://www.goalcast.com/serena-williams-overcome-obstacles-make-history/.

Williams, Serena. "'We Must Continue to Dream Big': An Open Letter from Serena Williams." *The Guardian*, November 29, 2016. https://www.theguardian.com/lifeandstyle/2016/nov/29/dream-big-open-letter-serena-williams-porter-magazine-incredible-women-of-2016-issue-women-athletes.

TAYLOR SWIFT

Associated Press. "Taylor Swift on Her Love of Reading & Writing: 'What If I End Up Writing a Script or a Book?'" *Billboard*, October 29, 2014. https://www.billboard.com/articles/columns/pop-shop/6297043/taylor-swift-on-her-love-of-reading-writing-what-if-i-end-up.

Billboard Staff. "Taylor Swift Dates Sell Out in Minutes." *Billboard*, October 26, 2009. https://www.billboard.com/articles/news/266942/taylor-swift-dates-sell-out-in-minutes.

Cerézo, Arvyn. "Why Taylor Swift Needs to Read Diverse Books." *Book Riot*, September 15, 2020. https://bookriot.com/taylor-swift-needs-to-read-diverse-books/.

Demarest, Abigail Abesamis. "13 Things You Probably Didn't Know about Taylor Swift." *Insider*, December 13, 2020. https://www.insider.com/things-you-didnt-know-about-taylor-swift-fun-facts-2019-1.

Dickey, Jack. "Taylor Swift on '1989,' Spotify, Her Next Tour, and Female Role Models." *Time*, November 13, 2014. https://time.com/3578249/taylor-swift-interview/.

Fox, Courtney. "Taylor Swift Grew Up on a Christmas Tree Farm in Pennsylvania." *Wide Open Country*, December 11, 2021. https://www.wideopencountry.com/taylor-swift-christmas-tree-farm/.

Grady, Kitty. "The Rise of the 'Lowercase Girl.'" *Vice*, August 28, 2020. https://www.vice.com/en/article/y3z45v/internet-lowercase-spelling-taylor-swift-charli-xcx.

Jepson, Louisa. *Taylor Swift*. New York: Simon & Schuster, 2013.

REFERENCES

Lu, Jimmy. "All the Literary References in Taylor Swift Songs." *NYC Tastemakers*, June 23, 2021. https://nyctastemakers.com/all-the-literary-references-in-taylor-swift-songs/.

McKinney, Kelsey. "John Green, Author of *A Fault in Our Stars*, Is Taylor Swift's Favorite Author." *Vox*, October 27, 2014. https://www.vox.com/xpress/2014/10/27/7079387 /taylor-swift-favorite-author-john-green.

"Taylor Swift." *Biography*, February 16, 2018. https://www.biography.com/musician/taylor-swift.

Vinson, Christina. "Taylor Swift Is Inspired by More Than Love in Her Songwriting." *Taste of Country*, March 28, 2013. https://tasteofcountry.com/taylor-swift-writing-inspiration/.

MALALA YOUSAFZAI

Dodson, P. Claire. "Malala Yousafzai's November Book Club Pick Is 'The Dancing Girls of Lahore.'" *Teen Vogue*, October 15, 2020. https://www.teenvogue.com/story/malala-yousafzai -november-book-club-pick-the-dancing-girls-of-lahore.

Halligan, Katherine. *Herstory: 50 Women and Girls Who Shook Up the World*. New York: Simon & Schuster Books for Young Readers, 2018.

Kovan, Brianna. "Malala Has the Best Book Recommendations, Obviously." *Bustle*, August 19, 2020. https://www.bustle.com/rule-breakers/malala-book-club-recommendation.

Malala Fund. Website: https://malala.org/malalas-story.

"Malala on Her Favorite Book." Video, *New York Times*, October 10, 2014. https://www.nytimes.com/video/world/asia/100000003169089/malala-on-her-favorite-book .html.

Van Gilder Cooke, Sonia. "Pakistani Heroine: How Malala Yousafzai Emerged from Anonymity." *Time*, October 23, 2012. https://world.time.com/2012/10/23/pakistani-heroine -how-malala-yousafzai-emerged-from-anonymity/#ixzz2YYXKTV4x.

Walsh, Jenni L. *She Dared: Malala Yousafzai*. New York: Scholastic, 2019.

Yousafzai, Malala. *I Am Malala: The Girl Who Stood Up for Education and Was Shot by the Taliban*. New York: Little, Brown and Company, 2013.

AMANDA GORMAN

Borgert-Spaniol, Megan. *Amanda Gorman*. Minneapolis, MN: Abdo Publishing, 2022.

Clarke, Rebecca. "Amanda Gorman, the Inaugural Poet Who Dreams of Writing Novels." *New York Times*, December 9, 2021. https://www.nytimes.com/2021/12/09/books/review/amanda -gorman-by-the-book-interview.html.

Drinks, Tara. "Amanda Gorman, Youth Poet Laureate, Has Speech and Auditory Processing Issues." Understood.org, July 24, 2018. https://www.understood.org/articles/en/amanda-gorman-youth-poet-laureate-has-speech-and-auditory-processing-issues.

Fink, David. "What Amanda Gorman Can Teach Everyone about Passing the Mic." *Age of Awareness*, February 7, 2021. https://medium.com/age-of-awareness/what-amanda-gorman-can-teach-everyone-about-passing-the-mic-d7925b2b0e89.

Funk, Katherine. "Amanda Gorman, Inauguration Poet, Wants to Be President One Day." *Newsweek*, January 20, 2021. https://www.newsweek.com/amanda-gorman-inauguration-poet-wants-president-one-day-1563170.

Hansen, Grace. *Amanda Gorman: Poet & Activist*. Minneapolis, MN: Abdo Publishing, 2021.

Jones, Meghan. "Meet Amanda Gorman: The History-Making Poet the World Is Still Talking About." *Reader's Digest*, April 27, 2021. https://www.rd.com/article/who-is-amanda-gorman/.

Miller, Korin. "Inaugural Poet Amanda Gorman Has Speech and Auditory Processing Disorders—Here's What That Means." *Health*, January 21, 2021. https://www.health.com/mind-body/amanda-gorman-speech-auditory-processing-disorder.

Obama, Michelle. "'Unity with Purpose.' Amanda Gorman and Michelle Obama Discuss Art, Identity, and Optimism." *Time*, February 4, 2021. https://time.com/5933596/amanda-gorman-michelle-obama-interview/.

Radin, Sara. "The First Youth Poet Laureate, Amanda Gorman Wants You to Know Her Work Goes Beyond Words." *Observer*, April 9, 2019. https://observer.com/2019/04/amanda-gorman-youth-poet-laureate-future-projects-women-in-the-world-summit/.

St. Felix, Doreen. "The Rise and Rise of Amanda Gorman." *Vogue*, April 7, 2021. https://www.vogue.com/article/amanda-gorman-cover-may-2021.

Stump, Scott. "Amanda Gorman Explains Why She Plans to Run for President in 2036." *Today*, September 21, 2021. https://www.today.com/news/news/amanda-gorman-explains-plans-run-president-2036-rcna2128.

Stutman, Michael. "Amanda Gorman—Using Her Special Gifts to Transform the World!" InspireMyKids.com, 2020. https://inspiremykids.com/amanda-gorman-using-her-special-gifts-to-transform-the-world/.

REFERENCES

MARLEY DIAS

"About Me." Marley Dias website: https://www.marleydias.com/about/.

Clift, Cortney, and Kat Armstrong. "Marley Dias Is Making the Literary World a Little More Colorful." Brit + Co., October 1, 2018. https://www.brit.co /marley-dias-future-women-of-america/.

Dias, Marley. *Marley Dias Gets It Done and So Can You!* New York: Scholastic, 2018.

Germain, Tabie. "2021 Soul Train Awards: 5 Things to Know about 'Souls of Justice' Honoree Marley Dias." BET, November 22, 2021. https://www.bet.com/article/1s5i2y /soul-train-awards-2021-5-things-to-know-about-marley-dias.

Katzman, Rebecca. "5 Questions for Marley Dias." *Time for Kids*, November 6, 2017. https://www.timeforkids.com/g34/5-questions-marley/.

Khan, Coco. "'They Just Wanted Us to Read about a White Boy and His Dog': Why Teenager Marley Dias Fought Back." *The Guardian*, August 28, 2019. https://www.theguardian.com /books/2019/aug/28/they-just-wanted-us-to-read-about-a-white-boy-and-his-dog-why-teenager -marley-dias-fought-back.

Labouvier, Chaedria. "This Is Marley Dias. She's 11. And She's on a Mission to Change the Publishing Industry." *Elle*, January 27, 2016. https://www.elle.com/culture/books/news/a33568 /marley-dias-1000blackgirlbooks-interview/.

Lyons, Sierra. "Marley Dias on Her Female Heroes, Representation, and Changing the World." *Teen Vogue*, March 2, 2021. https://www.teenvogue.com/story/marley-dias-female-heroes.

McGrath, Maggie. "From Activist to Author: How 12-Year-Old Marley Dias Is Changing the Face of Children's Literature." *Forbes*, June 13, 2017. https://www.forbes.com/sites/maggiemc grath/2017/06/13/from-activist-to-author-how-12-year-old-marley-dias-is-changing-the-face-of -childrens-literature/?sh=5bc849964ce0.

Stevens, Heidi. "Marley Dias, the Brains Behind #1000BlackGirlBooks, Is Touring with a Book of Her Own." *Chicago Tribune*, January 30, 2018. https://www.chicagotribune.com/columns/heidi-stevens /ct-life-stevens-tuesday-marley-dias-book-appearances-0130-story.html.

KATHLEEN KRULL

Halverson, Deborah. "On Revision: Kathleen Krull, in Memoriam." DeadEditor.com, January 19, 2021. https://www.deareditor.com/2021/01 /on-revision-kathleen-krull-in-memoriam/.

Maughan, Shannon. "Obituary: Kathleen Krull." *Publishers Weekly*, January 20, 2021. https://www.publishersweekly.com/pw/by-topic/childrens/childrens-authors/article/85350 -obituary-kathleen-krull.html.

Simons, Rani and Devi. "Interview: Kathleen Krull." *Philadelphia Stories*, May 20, 2019. https:// philadelphiastories.org/article/interview-kathleen-krull/.

"A Video Interview with Kathleen Krull." *Reading Rockets*. https://www.readingrockets.org /books/interviews/krull.

MORE GIRLS WITH BOOKS

Baker, Jean H. *Margaret Sanger: A Life of Passion*. New York: Hill & Wang, 2011.

Blewett, Kelly. "Ursula Nordstrom and the Queer History of the Children's Book." *Los Angeles Review of Books*, August 28, 2016. https://lareviewofbooks.org/article/ursula -nordstrom-and-the-queer-history-of-the-childrens-book/.

Brechka, Frank T. "Catherine the Great: The Books She Read." *Journal of Library History (1966– 1972)* 4, no. 1 (January 1969): 39–52. http://www.jstor.org/stable/25540141.

Bridges, Ruby. *Through My Eyes*. New York: Scholastic, 1999.

Bush, Laura. "Mrs. Bush's Remarks at Laura Bush Foundation for America's Libraries Grant Awards." White House Archives: President George W. Bush, May 20, 2003. https://georgewbush-whitehouse.archives.gov/news/releases/2003/05/20030520-17.html.

Bush, Laura. *Spoken from the Heart*. New York: Simon & Schuster, 2010.

Doak, Robin S. *Dolores Huerta: Labor Leader and Civil Rights Activist*. Minneapolis, MN: Compass Point, 2008.

Frank, Anne. *The Diary of a Young Girl: The Definitive Edition*. New York: Knopf, 2010.

Hansen, Joyce A. *Mary McLeod Bethune and Black Women's Political Activism*. Columbia: University of Missouri Press, 2003.

Kramer, Rita. *Maria Montessori*. New York: Putnam, 1976.

Krull, Kathleen. *A Kids' Guide to America's First Ladies*. New York: HarperCollins, 2017.

Krull, Kathleen. *Lives of the Writers: Comedies, Tragedies (and What the Neighbors Thought)*. Boston: HMH Books for Young Readers, 2014

Krull, Kathleen. *Louisa May's Battle: How the Civil War Led to Little Women*. New York: Bloomsbury, 2013.

Krull, Kathleen. *Marie Curie*. New York: Penguin Young Readers Groups, 2009.

REFERENCES

Krull, Kathleen. *Women Who Broke the Rules: Judy Blume*. New York: Bloomsbury, 2015.

Lareau, Louise. "NYPL's Anne Carroll Moore: A Pioneer Who Opened Library Doors to Kids . . . Literally." New York Public Library, March 8, 2021. https://www.nypl.org/blog/2021/03/08/nypls-anne-carroll-moore-a-pioneer-who-opened-library-doors-to-kids.

Leaming, Barbara. *Jacqueline Bouvier Kennedy Onassis: The Untold Story*. New York: St. Martin's, 2014.

Ling, Bettina. *Maya Lin*. Austin, TX: Raintree Steck-Vaughn, 1997.

Maddocks, Fiona. *Hildegard of Bingen: The Woman of Her Age*. New York: Doubleday, 2001.

Marcus, Leonard, ed. *Dear Genius: The Letters of Ursula Nordstrom*. New York: HarperCollins, 1998.

Marshall, Megan. *Margaret Fuller: A New American Life*. Boston: Houghton Mifflin, 2013.

Meador, Betty De Shong. *Inanna, Lady of Largest Heart: Poems of the Sumerian High Priestess Enheduanna*. Austin: University of Texas, 2000.

Obama, Michelle. *Becoming*. New York: Crown, 2021.

Perlingieri, Ilya Sandra. *Sofonisba Anguissola: The First Great Woman Artist of the Renaissance*. New York: Rizzoli, 1992.

Pittman, Taylor. "Michelle Obama Shares the Children's Books She Used to Read to Her Daughters." HuffPost, March 7, 2019. https://www.huffpost.com/entry/michelle-obama-childrens-books_l_5c815a69e4b020b54d832f1d.

Sayers, Francis Clarke. *Anne Carroll Moore*. New York: Atheneum, 1972.

Seward, Desmond. *Eleanor of Aquitaine: The Mother Queen*. London: David & Charles, 1978.

Tyler, Royall. "Murasaki Shikibu: Brief Life of a Legendary Novelist." *Harvard Magazine*, May–June 2002. https://www.harvardmagazine.com/2002/05/murasaki-shikibu.html.

Wagner-Martin, Linda. *Favored Strangers: Gertrude Stein and Her Family*. New Brunswick, NJ: Rutgers University Press, 1995.

INDEX

INDEX